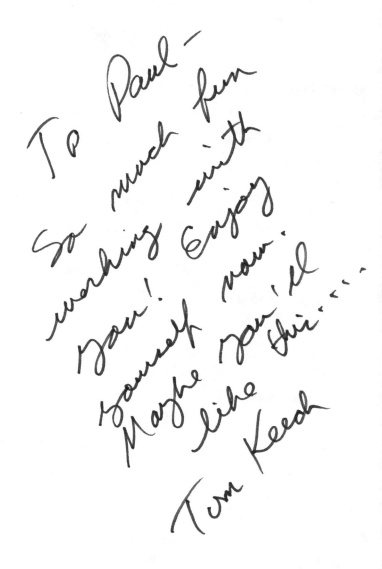

To Paul —
So much fun
working with
you! Enjoy
yourself now.
Maybe you'll
like this....

Tom Keeda

by
Thomas W. Keech

Real
Nice Books, LLC
Baltimore, 2011

ISBN 978-0-9836990-0-2

Published by
Real Nice Books, LLC
11 Dutton Court
Baltimore, Maryland 21228

1 3 5 7 9 10 8 6 4 2

*Publisher's note: This is a work of fiction. Names, characters, places,
institutions and incidents are entirely the product of the author's
imagination or are used fictitiously, and any resemblance to actual
persons, living or dead, or to events, incidents, institutions or places
is entirely coincidental.*

Printed in the U.S.A.

Set in Sabon.
Interior book design by Kate Boyer - Heron and Earth Design
Cover art and design by Vanessa Snyder

For Sharon

Also by Thomas Keech
The Crawlspace Conspiracy

Prey for Love

Chapter 1

Dad drops me off in his minivan, as if I can't walk now, as if I'm some kind of cripple since it happened. Inside that madhouse of a school, Mr. Folsom is already putting math problems on the board. He's so excited his chalk-stained hand quivers and makes extra squiggles on the equations. Mr. Folsom's hair is twisted grey and brown, cut in a rough bowl in back that would be okay if it were two inches shorter and on a girl. Mom said a lot of things in the past two days to explain to me why she was leaving. I'm sure they're all preserved in amber in my brain somewhere, and maybe I'll analyze them years from now when I might need to figure out why I was such a loser as a kid.

Every time Mr. Folsom turns around, his eyes sweep the room desperately, searching for another demented math brain like his. I always look down. Mr. Folsom's never been married. He says he's married to math. Math will put us all on the moon, he says – but everybody knows there's nothing up there, and he still has to show up at this school every day where the kids all act so bored, and I see him every Monday morning in the teachers' lounge with his face in his hands. Mom told me, girl to girl, that she was leaving for love. My legs feel funny again this morning, all tingling and hollow, and I have to step one foot carefully in front of the other just to keep my balance. Like a cripple. Or like I'm already on the moon.

Johnson is a truly certified moron or cripple of some kind.

They brought him to our class the second day of school. So he's like in this ninth-grade algebra class and can barely write his name. They won't tell us what's wrong with him. We're supposed to think that he's just "different," I guess like he just has a previously unknown color of hair or something. His mother came into the class one day in that first week and told us he was the same as any of us. I thought that was the biggest lie that had ever been told in that school, but it turns out it wasn't even close. Johnson has big, sad eyes, but if I look at him for more than a second he reaches out and tries to touch my shirt.

So I balance my way down the hall in my moonwalk so slowly I come in late and have to sit next to Johnson. No regular kid wants to. The last regular kid who comes into the classroom has to sit right next to him and fight off getting sprayed or groped. Lucky gets to school early just so he can watch everybody scrambling not to be in the seat next to Johnson. Lucky calls it Spit Musical Chairs.

Mom called me last night.

"I'm disappointed in how you're taking this."

"Disappointed?"

"You're supposed to go to your classes instead of hanging around drinking in the woods."

"How did you know that?"

"I keep track. I care about you, Kate."

"But you're leaving us."

"I'm leaving your father."

"Do you want me to come live with you and Anton?"

She took such a long time thinking up an answer I didn't bother to listen when it came.

"You can meet some nice people in the woods, Mom. You'd be surprised."

"Don't be juvenile, Kate."

"Like you're so grown up, Mom, running off with that cretin."

For a year she's been going to "work" on Saturday nights, dressed like somebody her age would dress for a date. Once, last year, I stood in front of her at the front door and asked her where she was really going. Dad came over and saw us, but then he just turned his back and tried to walk away. I screamed for him to come back. He did turn around, but then he just stared at her like he was in some kind of trance, and she stared back at him for a minute and then left anyway. Then he went upstairs without talking to me. It's like I cracked the house apart just then. She went out one way and he went out the other, and I was standing in the middle, but really nowhere. For a whole year I still pretended to be normal whenever I went outside of the house. Diane hadn't moved back yet, and so I tried to make new friends at school, but everybody was in some group of their own.

I spent all my nights last year in my room, reading my schoolbooks over and over like they would have some clue for holding my family together. After midnight, I'd get into bed and try to think of happy old things like Mom's stories of Grandma out in the country years ago, stories filled with scrub boards and water pails and bibles. But I was afraid to fall asleep. When I fell asleep I'd always dream that I was still there in my bed, but I would be all alone and the house would be dead quiet and I couldn't move, and then everything would go so black it seemed like I didn't have any eyes, and I would be lying there blind and numb and frozen like I was already dead. When I woke up, I always made a lot of noise, and my parents each started giving me separate lectures about drugs.

Last summer, Mom tried to force me to work in Anton's office with her. Anton has short, blond hair curled down in a little fringe over his forehead, and his face has a yellowish chemical tan all year long. He wears tight shirts to show off his disgusting middle-aged muscles, and a big diamond earring. Dad told me Anton inherited the company from his father. His father

sold most of the lots in Glenwood when it was first developed. My father says that Anton's father must have done a good job, because everybody still uses the same company. Dad says Anton's been rich since he was a kid and he's never done anything but get drunk and speed around Glenwood in the fast cars his father bought him. I can hear Anton's car all the time on the streets. His car has artwork on it so you can't miss him coming even if you're deaf.

Mr. Folsom explains the equations he just put on the board. If a house on one quarter of an acre of land would net x dollars, and a house on one-third acre would net y dollars, and an acre of land costs z dollars, what number of houses per acre would yield the maximum profit? Mr. Folsom's high voice is shaking with excitement over how you can solve these equations, and he turns around to face us with such a happy look in his eyes. But nobody cares.

Diane was the only one who could make me see what was happening. It was on my fourteenth birthday, a few months ago. When we were kids, they would drive us to gymnastics together. We were always laughing the whole way. Then she moved away, and when she came back to Glenwood a few years later, things were not so hilarious any more. I didn't feel like performing tricks for grownups any more. My mother and I were screaming at each other all the time, and Dad was off hiding in a corner. The strange thing was, Mom was the one who actually made me invite Diane to my fourteenth birthday. I thought she was trying to repair me socially.

Diane was taller than me and her hair was dyed purple and she chased boy after boy until she got them interested – then she dumped them. She showed up right on time for the party. Dad called us in to the living room and had us sit down on the sofa across from him. He had this weird kind of fake smile on his face.

"So, Mr. Alexander, you've got Kate's new Mustang

convertible tied up with a red ribbon in the garage, right?"

Of course, we don't even have a garage, just a carport.

I heard Mom's car pull up in the driveway and stop under the carport just then, but Dad didn't seem to notice. He went into the kitchen and brought out a little bakery cake with fourteen candles on it.

"We got you a little present. It's no big deal. With the money we saved on this one, we can buy you that Mustang on your sixteenth birthday," he laughed, "or maybe, at the rate we're going, your sixtieth."

He pulled a small package out from his shirt pocket. Just as he was handing it to me, Mom stepped in behind him from the kitchen wearing one of her beige suits. Dad jumped when he heard her behind him. Mom jerked to a stop herself, like she was surprised by something too. Her face got red and she looked back and forth between Diane and me. There was this cold, icky feeling in the room.

"I was just giving Kate her present," Dad said, without looking at Mom.

"Oh, good, but let's light the candles first," Mom said in her usual honey-coated, efficient voice. Dad clapped himself on the head like he was dumb, and ran into the kitchen to get matches. While he was lighting the candles, Mom said, "We have another present for you." She pulled a tiny wrapped box out of her pocketbook and put it on the table next to the cake. Dad's hand stopped for a second over the candles, and he jerked it back like he had burned himself.

"That's the keys to the Mustang. See? We're working on it bit by bit." Dad was still rubbing his hand to get the burn off. It wasn't too good a joke since the box was way too small to hold even keys. Anyone could see it was a jewelry box, but he had no clue what jewelry was in it.

I pointed to the birthday present Dad had just handed me.

"I want to open that one first." It was an iPod. The other

present, in the tiny box that my mother brought, was a gold pin in the shape of a heart outlined in tiny diamonds.

"Thanks. Thanks for both of these things."

"We know you deserve much more. You're such a great girl." Dad sounded like he was about ready to cry.

"Yes. Your father's right." Mom was forced to say it. The room seemed so hollow. It was like their words were coming out a little ways into the air and then just falling down on the carpet between us. Mom and Dad tried to start up the joking with Diane again, but they were each having their own conversation with her. Each one acted like the other wasn't there.

"Thanks. Thanks for these." My words fell into the hole in the middle of the room.

Then I knew why Diane had been invited. So I couldn't scream.

"The car – that's no problem," Diane teased. "Kate's boyfriend – you know, the twenty-five-year-old guy you haven't met – he lets her drive his Viper all the time."

"Oh, I hear that you have a lot of boyfriends," Dad tried to tease back.

"Never enough."

She pulled a small box, beautifully wrapped in blue and white, out of her pocketbook. It was a set of letter paper and envelopes, white, with my name printed on top in the middle of a starlit sky.

"Remember when we were little, we used to lie in hammocks in the back yard at night and make up our own constellations, with our own names?"

"I could never forget that."

I'll never forget you. Diane touched me on the arm. My parents just sat there with their fake smiles on their faces.

"Let's go out in the kitchen." I begged her with my eyes to say yes. Out of their sight in the kitchen, Diane and I started gossiping about our friends again like those years apart hadn't

happened; but then she froze. She was leaning down and looking into the refrigerator. When I looked, she waved her hand for me to come over. She showed me a big white box in the refrigerator, a cake box. Mom had gotten me one too. I nodded and turned away, but Diane wouldn't stop. She pulled the box out and set it on the counter and slowly pulled off the string and tape that held it together. The sound of that tape being ripped off the cardboard practically echoed in the dead quiet of the house.

After she efficiently opened the flaps and top, we saw what we expected, another bakery cake, this one with white icing and pink hearts and pink tracing that read, "Happy Birthday Kate from Mom and Dad."

"My God, Kate," she whispered. "You have two completely separate birthday parties in the same house! I was going to take this out to the living room for a joke. But this isn't funny, is it?"

Johnson's hair is cut in rough bangs that fall halfway down his forehead. His head is extra large, the skin around his mouth is chapped from always being wet, and his face is bruised and scabbed from hitting himself and banging his head on everything. He usually has a guard, a black lady with a sour face who's always wrestling with him, but she isn't here today.

He's trying to look at me with those sad brown eyes. I bunch my hair up on that side of my face so he can't. But then I'm wondering what he's doing, so I sneak a peek. My one eye meets his, and we both laugh. Then he wants to touch my hair. He's got a thing for me so bad his hand is shaking. I push his hand away but he grabs mine. It probably looks like we're holding hands, so then I want to die. Somebody laughs and Mr. Folsom sees what's happening and comes over fast and cracks a book down so hard on Johnson's desk that Johnson lets go. But then it's Mr. Folsom who's shaking, looking at us kids like he's done something wrong and he's hoping we won't tell.

Diane and I start hanging around with each other again after that party. Now she lives in a much newer house on the other side of Glenwood. She's taller and richer and cooler than me, and she's not afraid of anything. She never mentions my sickening birthday party. One day she asks me to go down to the woods after school.

It's a gorgeous day. The trail is paved like a road and it runs from the very back of the school soccer field all the way down the woods to the stream. Then it goes across the stream, then I guess even further. Kids always talk about skateboarding there after dark. Losers. We escape down the trail by ourselves. These woods are amazing. Sunlight slices through the trees, lighting up meadows of scarlet berries on one side, carpets of green fern on the other. A little tree holds its blackened hands out to us, fingers upturned, with poisonous-looking berries at the tip of each one. Diane's purple hair flashes in and out of the sun. Giant trees sway overhead and creak like old houses.

Diane shows me the hangout, a little depression in the woods just out of sight of the trail. You have to get off the trail and twist through a lot of thick brown vines, then dodge through a school of skinny saplings. They seem like they're begging for the little bit of sun that makes it down here through the fully-grown trees. Kids are hanging out at the far edge, in the shade. The floor is covered with high grass and tangled bushes, all overlaid with twisting vines and speckled with leaves.

Diane and I walk right across the depression toward the guys on the other side. I don't know any of them.

"What are you guys drinking?" she calls out.

"Wine coolers."

"Got some for us?"

She acts like she's done this a thousand times before. The scariest one, the one Diane calls Rat, doesn't say anything. He's skinny, with a blond buzz cut and a stubbly beard. He has scabs all over his hands and arms, and the letters "F-U-C-K" written

on his forearm in a ball-point-pen tattoo.

"Got any money?" one of the other boys says.

I look at Diane.

"Do you take American Express?"

We sit down a little ways away. The deep green grass here looks like it has just been flattened down by elephants. The boys are sitting with their backs against trees. The sun cuts sharp shadows on the ground. Dying vines with orange and yellow berries bob in the breeze. The boys just keep drinking and yelling out to each other about how high they're getting.

"What should we do?'

Diane gets this great look in her eyes.

"This is a bust. Let's go to my house. It's like, do whatever you want there. My sister turned twelve and my parents are never at home any more."

She stands up, tossing her hair.

"What would you girls like to drink?" It's Rat, yelling over at us. His voice is really deep for somebody so skinny and scabby, but he sounds like he's faking he's a host at some old people's cocktail party and we're neighbors from down the street. Diane catches my eye.

"Wine coolers."

They taste like peach soda, only with a sharpness underneath. I'm nervous and drink in gulps, stopping after each swallow to look at Diane to check out if anything has happened yet. She's lying in the grass, sipping slowly and swinging the bottle back and forth lazily, looking up at the sky. It's now raining giant yellow leaves as big as plates.

"Ms. Nesbitt is right. This is a beautiful planet."

"This place is so wasted on these morons."

Rat hears only one word. "Wasted! Yeah, we're all gonna get wasted!"

I gulp down two bottles and start on another. Little by little I can feel a wild, sweet spirit being unlocked inside me. It's like I

remember just in time that I'm okay, that we're all okay. There's a confusing happiness all around. Everything is slower and funnier. I pick up one of the big yellow leaves and show Diane the green veins branching through it. I try to tell her how beautiful it looks to me. The boys crack up at the way I'm talking. I knock my bottle over, but Rat hands me another one right away. The boys are making me laugh and I can't stop.

I'm holding my bottle with two hands like a baby and can't look at Diane because I'm laughing so hard I'm afraid I'll pee my pants. She spills her bottle too, and we both just laugh. We're both lying back and feeling at peace with the green life beneath us and reaching up and trying to catch the leaves swirling down. Then everything starts swirling.

"Diane, I feel awful."

Diane crawls over and forces me to sit up. Soon I'm retching right onto the ground. Then the boys start acting nice, saying it won't last long. It's like I'm sick, but it is an honorable sickness, and they have it too, and I am now one of them. My head is pounding too, and I'd rather be anywhere else, but what the boys are saying is kind of true. We have all sunk down together, and we're all flattened here under a layer of alcohol, staring at each other like mutant deep-water fish at the very bottom of the sea.

Then I see Lucky stalking across the little depression towards us. I've known him since the fourth grade and I used to like him when I was little, but I haven't talked to him in a couple of years. His head is shaved, making his dark eyes seem even larger. He wears a silver earring. Diane, Lucky and I worked together on a group project once, making a model of a Mayan or a Lithuanian village or something. He got all the materials from his father, who got them from a construction site. All that I remember about the project was that he made it fun.

"Oh God, Diane. He's gonna think I'm such a loser!"

"Loser, Schmoozer. Hey, Lucky!"

When I open my eyes he's parting the last of the vines at the edges of the depression and sitting down next to me, right between me and Rat.

Rat sits up like he's been bitten by a snake.

"I saw you with that cop, Corporal Walton. How do I know you're not working for them?"

"You don't."

Then Rat jumps up and they both stand with their chests out toward each other like two gorillas. Lucky's pretty big and isn't so skinny as Rat. I look up and get this dizzy view of the two of them facing off.

Then Rat pulls out a knife. He twists it slowly so the sun reflects in Lucky's eyes.

"I can cut you up, you smart-ass."

"Oh yeah, like you're going to kill me or something. Why don't you just chill, Rat?"

"You were tight with me last summer when you wanted me to get you beer. Now you're sucking up to the cops."

"If you're going to do something, do something. Or else just leave me alone."

I can't hold my head up any more, but I can hear them edge around each other. Then they stop, like they've run out of tough-guy things to say. Diane and the other guys are dead quiet. The woods go so quiet I can hear the giant leaves clattering their way down through the trees. My head starts to pound again and I close my eyes. Nothing happens for a long time; then I hear footsteps going away through the brush. I open my eyes and it's just Lucky and me. He looks at me. Then I throw up.

"If you lie on your back like that, you could choke on your own puke."

It's all I can do to keep from getting stuff on him.

"Dying doesn't seem so bad right now."

"Don't talk." He holds me, cupping my forehead in his hand – face down, so I won't choke. He holds my hair back with his

other hand. Thank God he can't see my face. The only thing I can see is the forest floor of leaves and vines spinning around. My cheek pushes against the denim of his jeans.

"This is my first time. I'm sorry."

"Diane told me what happened to you. About your mother."

"Don't make me think about that witch."

"Kate, it happens to everybody. Everything that's happening to you, it happens to everybody."

"It happened to you?"

Then I pass out or fall asleep because the next thing I notice it's colder and the sunlight is gone from the forest floor. We are still all alone. I've been lying across his legs like a rag doll. I push myself up. I'm not dizzy any more, but my head is pounding.

"You said something happened to you. What was it?" This is the first thing I say, like my brain was thinking about him all the time I was passed out.

He shakes his head and a shudder runs through him. His earring flashes. But he doesn't answer. Instead he pushes back my hair and straightens it. I start to feel safe that nothing else will come up out of my stomach, so I lie on my side, in the brush, facing him. Still, he doesn't answer. He feels more comfortable, I can tell, cleaning me up than talking. Those dark brown eyes are holding something back. I know that I should not take his stony silence for an answer. In a way, he is already mine, and I know that he should tell me. And then I know that he will. Unlike Rat, I will win my face-off with Lucky.

Diane left my birthday party soon after we discovered that second cake. I lay out on the grass of the front lawn, crying. The sky above me faded, it's pink swatches of color slowly turning to violet, the edges of the clouds glowing like silver threads. At the end of our driveway, there was a little yellow flame-shaped bulb set on a ivy-covered pole shaped like a candle. It lit up just

as the lawns and trees on the street faded into a dim green blur. I walked around to the side of the house. I knew I'd see Mom getting into her car, getting ready to go. She stopped and stood there when she saw me coming.

The side door to the house opened, and Dad stepped down to the concrete pad under the carport. Mom let out a big sigh and let her arm go limp, and her pocketbook thumped against the car door. Dad just stood there, not saying anything.

"You're leaving again?"

"I'm due back at the office, Kate. I'm doing a settlement tomorrow at eight in the morning."

"Why couldn't you finish it before?"

"I tried, Kate. I had to leave early. This party. I had to pick up your pin."

She rolled the leather strap around her fingers until the pocketbook was clutched in her hand, then looked out past the little candle at the end of the driveway. Mom is better looking than I'll ever be. We both have blonde hair, but hers is sculpted and looks so smart while mine just hangs in a thick mop that I can't do anything with. She always says I don't have the face for the sculpted look anyway, and I guess that's supposed to cheer me up. She has that delicate nose and those high cheekbones that make her look so classy. Her beauty is in the shape of her face, and it's still there in the deep twilight. People say my own green eyes are beautiful and my smile is cute. That's about it.

I had the heart pin in my hand, its diamonds sparkling like tiny cat's eyes in the weak light from the lamppost.

"Do you really have to go?" Dad blurted out.

"Yes, Sam." She said this softly like she was talking to a child. He didn't say anything, just looked down into the darkness under the car. Then he reached out his hand toward me for the pin.

"It's beautiful." He was no longer pretending to have seen it before. Mom and I watched him run his thumb very slowly

around the heart-shaped outline of diamonds. Then he put it back in my hand. "I'll leave the two of you alone."

He went inside. The screen door slowly hissed closed, the latch clicking loudly in the stillness.

"Why are you going?"

"Kate, I just told you."

"You know what I mean."

"Kate, these things happen. It's not anybody's fault."

She pulled at the door handle of her car.

"It's somebody's fault." My voice came out loud. "You can't stand me. Why don't you just admit it?"

The car door opened and the interior lights came on behind her. I could see her face only in silhouette. It seemed like a long time before she answered. "I don't dislike you, Kate." I knew she was holding herself back from adding up all the reasons she should. "I'm so tired. Tired of all this." Then she got in the car, started the engine, drove fast down the driveway and squealed into the street like she couldn't wait to be out of my sight.

I walked down the driveway and out to the street. The moon had started to sail up over the low houses at the end of our block. On the sidewalk, a few blocks from our house, you could still see traces of an environmental project I did in the sixth grade. We took stencils and painted "Chesapeake Bay Input" in green on the cement cover of every storm drain in the development. After my mother drove away that night I threw that diamond pin down the storm drain, hoping some huge bluefish would eat up my sparkling heart, or some crab would get it tangled in its claws so some waterman's child could find it in the soft coral rays of the dawn.

Johnson's fingernails are all bitten down, and the back of his hand is covered with scribbles. Class is over and people are getting up and walking out of the room. I look over at him and he stares back at me like some kind of sad puppy. He has a paper

14

in his hand, and he's drawn a heart on it in red felt marker. I can see inside the heart where he's made the letters "K-A-T." At first I don't get that this is supposed to be my name.

It must suck to be him, to be such a jittery cretin that the girls run away from you and the boys punch you every chance they get. Everyone else is gone, so I stand up. His whole body is shaking when he stands up. He seems like a little boy now, with his thick black hair piled on top of his head like it's been beaten with a greasy eggbeater. He's picking at his shirtsleeves but still holding the paper out to me in one hand.

"Thank you," I say. I figure he's such a love-struck retard he can't even hand it to me, so I take it from his fingers. Then I reach out and touch his disgusting face just because I know he would love that so much.

But as I'm turning around I feel his fingers in my hair.

"Kate!" Johnson talks in a mechanical, high-pitched voice that sounds like he learned to talk from watching cartoons.

"Okay. Don't do that!"

But now both of his hands are twisted in my hair and I'm backing up so fast I corner myself at the back of the room. He bangs my head into the wall so hard everything goes white, and when I come to he's behind me, grabbing at my breasts and rubbing himself against me. He's way too strong.

"Wait." My face is pushed into the wall. "Wait. Don't you like me?"

No answer. I try to curl myself into a ball, but he's all over me. I can smell his stale medication breath. He's clawing at my breasts. I bend his fingers back and get one of his hands off, then twist around so he's not humping me anymore, but I can't get the other hand off. Then he's behind me again.

"Randy, don't you like me? Let me turn around."

"Kiss."

My stomach heaves.

"No."

He slams me into the corner again. He doesn't even know what to do. So he's trying everything.

"Okay, Randy. Turn me around."

There's a super-loud moan right in my ear.

"Turn me around. I'll kiss you."

Then his hands drop off. He turns me around and pushes his face right up to mine. His eyes are wild, and he can't stop humping against me, but he's holding back that slobbery face, catching his breath, waiting for me.

I put my hands on both sides of his face and push him back gently. His whole body is shaking, but he lets me do this, and I imagine his eyes are going soft. My heart is jolting and I don't know what to do. Then, the instant he's off me and he can't hump me any more, he starts shaking and moaning and trying to push into me again. I only have a second, so I knee him in the crotch as hard as I can. He doubles up and screams and tries to lean against me, but I throw him down to the ground and run out of the classroom.

The hallway is almost deserted. I see the new principal, Mr. Freeland, at the end of the corridor, just outside the auditorium. I can hear the sound of my own hysterical breathing echoing off the concrete walls. No sound comes out when I try to scream. I run towards Mr. Freeland. He turns and stares down the hall at me, his eyebrows raised.

"Kate!" his voice booms out. "WALK!"

Chapter 2

We are not the only edge-of-the-woods animals, just the only ones who fear the instincts that drive us there. It should have been obvious during the last few years of my marriage that I had failed to pull up the roots that bound me too tightly to the past. That awful, insomniac humming of my nerves throughout those years of nights was the sound of those roots being ripped up by someone else. Had I the courage to walk with the grace of the deer from the deep forest through the ambiguous shade to the bright open field where there are no disguises, I might have been able to use the power of my dark forest dream to hold the only prey I ever wanted. When I won Clare's love I thought I had done just that, but that notion now seemed to be just another misty self-delusion burning off quickly under the glare of the harsh new sun. I was left exposed, caught out in the open with a job that was not really a job, a life dream that was more like a boy's fantasy – and still blindly in love with the woman who was going to tell me today that she was leaving for good.

"Don't steal too many hearts today."

Kate glanced back and gave me her fourteen-year-old, sweet-and-sour smile. She got out and walked resolutely away from the paternal minivan and toward the school, the spring in her step growing stronger with the distance. Her shift from tomboy to sexy had come too fast. She wore low-slung jeans and had the beginnings of a real figure, her lush blond hair puffing out

behind her in a thick ponytail. God help the young schoolboys who'd have to deal with that.

The curse of the missing parent had just been visited on another generation of Alexanders. My father died young, but my mother leavened that curse with surplus measures of so much love I could not just keep it to myself. I thought it was my heritage. But now, no matter what I tried, no matter what I denied, Clare was leaving Kate and me on purpose, just because she did not love us enough to stay.

The road home from the school bordered the woods, just a tiny slice of green on the edge of what had once been my grandfather's farm. My grandfather outlived my father, and I remember coming up from North Carolina once to visit his farm, stealing the eggs from the chickens, listening to his complicated and long-winded stories. My mother sold the rest of the farm to developers when I was a teenager, then eked out a living on a widow's financial plan that didn't extend any farther than me being twenty-two and graduating from college. I never quite made the graduating from college part, but before she died she saw Clare and I bound together in a love as sweet and deep as her own.

What was left of the farm was just a narrow strip of land covered with a virgin forest of hardwoods that ran down a long hill to the stream, a strip too steep and small to be of much use for farming or even development. After my mother left that little strip of woods to me, Clare and I used to dream of building a house there, raising our family on family land and passing it on to the next generation of Alexanders. I don't think we ever mentioned this dream to Kate – but the minute our family fell apart, Kate gravitated to those woods as if she were grasping for those roots herself.

There had been no disguising the joy in Clare's eyes on those evenings when she had to go out and prepare her real estate settlements. Over the past few years, she became more and more

absorbed in her work with her boss Anton, and she was home less and less. I knew she worked all those hours because she wanted a better life for us. And if something happened between her and Anton, it didn't happen on purpose.

Clare's blue Acura sparkled just up ahead in front of our house under a preternaturally white September sun. The leaves of the maple we had planted in our yard ten years ago burned crimson. I was at her side by the time she climbed out of her car. Her blonde hair was pulled back on both sides of her head and held with barrettes, girl-style. Her green pencil skirt with gold buttons at the slit reflected the color of her eyes. Her fitted white blouse pinned with a gold broach, her amber necklace, her beige high heels – it all served to remind me that I was in over my head.

"You look great. You're coming in, right?'

"Sam, I have to tell you something."

"I should tell you how Kate's doing."

The parent card. My last card. But it worked. She came in, sat down, even picked up the cup of coffee I had kept warm.

"She's not taking this well."

"I know. She has a whole list of derogatory terms for me. I can hear them on my answering machine any time I want."

"She's just a kid."

"Is this a guilt trip? Do you think this is all my fault?"

"No, no. She's having trouble not just with you ..."

"I don't think I'm the only bad guy." She rattled her cup back into its saucer. "I didn't want to leave her. I wanted to leave you. She can come with me. She's going to want things some day, Sam. I may not be able to afford them, but at least I'm going to try. You never even tried."

"I can buy her the things she needs."

"I'm not talking just about *things*, Sam. You're making me say this. She needs somebody who's not all ... twisted inside himself."

"I know." It was my fault. I'd been living in a dream world. But this was my last chance to get her out of hers. "It seems to me, Clare, that you're still making a horrible mistake."

"Sam, after all these years, I doubt if you know anything about me."

"I'm worried about you. What do you really know about Anton?"

"Sam, it's too late for this conversation."

She sat back and stared past me at the wall. She bit her lip as she always did when she was tense. When I caught her eye, she glanced down in a tiny, familiar gesture of guilt that made me catch my breath. This was the closest she'd let me come in a long time. I watched her face for any sign that this tiny seed of a feeling for me could grow.

We met sixteen years before on the evening after I had gained a few minutes of campus fame by running for the first – and, it turned out, the only – touchdown of my college football career at our small liberal arts school in the foothills of the North Carolina Appalachians. The coach generally alternated me with another guy at tailback, as if he couldn't decide which of us was worse. We had a good enough offensive line, at least on the left side, so there would usually be a hole I could slam myself through for two or three yards; but once through the line I didn't have enough speed to evade the linebackers, and so our coach had pretty much switched to a passing game. I was just the collision guy, and the pain turned to numbness, and this was a way to get through college without a father or any close friends.

But there was one magic play when a giant hole opened outside of left tackle and I had gained seven yards and was into the secondary before I knew what was happening. I still remember the instant that everything that had been so blocked up was so suddenly open. My body jumped with an instinctive leap to freedom. A linebacker, his head down a little too far, dove blindly at my ankles. I hopped to the side and he flew by,

and I stumbled forward a few more steps. The safety lunged for me, too fast, out of control, and I waited until the last instant, turned sideways and slipped his tackle. I looked up and saw a flash of green alleyway that was clear for all sixty yards to the end zone.

I saw a film later that showed how half of my team caught up with me and mowed down the rest of the opposing team's secondary, one by one; but I didn't remember seeing this. I did remember, and still do remember, the soft field, the bright green grass, the white lines flying by – and the sudden feeling that, for once, I would not screw up, and this thing was really going to work.

One extraordinary moment brought another. I saw her, short blonde hair, cheekbones, as she pulled on a sweater at an outdoor keg party after the game. She moved with an unconscious grace, deflecting the flirtatious leers of the players and surfing alone somewhere above the ambient current of ego and sex. There are days when you know that something is guiding you. I walked up to her. She turned and looked at me, really saw me with those steady green eyes, and I knew that my boyhood was over and this was where my real life would begin.

And this is where it would end. Sixteen years later, Clare lifted her eyes to me and brushed a stray curl off her cheek with a professional grace that signaled nothing but impatience. She was hardly looking at me. I have to admit there wasn't much to see anyway. Trying to smother any reaction she might find objectionable, I had pretty much erased myself. I would have been more honestly abject if I were down on my knees and begging.

The light glowing through the wide front window illuminated a bleak series of hard truths. Clare would live the rest of her life with someone else. She might have to talk to me once in a while about Kate, but she would never catch my eye and smile again. She would never be with me again. No matter what I did, she

was never coming back. Never. If there is a God, he is cruel beyond measure.

"Sam, the reason I'm here today ..."

"Wait a minute, honey."

The phone was ringing. I walked out of the living room to pick it up in the kitchen. It was Mrs. Cascio, the school secretary at Kate's school.

"I'm calling to see what would be a good time for you and Mrs. Alexander to come to a meeting at school with Principal Freeland and myself."

"What?"

"Kate's cut a lot of classes lately. We don't know where she's going. We're afraid there might be something wrong. We'd like to talk to you and Mrs. Alexander."

"Oh. I didn't know ..."

"What's that, Mr. Alexander?"

"Um, can we do this later? This is a very bad time. I promise I'll call, make an appointment, just ... not now."

I poured another cup of coffee and brought it out to Clare. My wife sat stock-still, didn't touch the cup, didn't lean toward it. She didn't ask me about the phone call. Her only interest in me was to politely get me out of her life. Having to go on living myself, knowing she was still alive, but with someone else, would be unbearable. The relentless compromises my heart would have to make to stay sane didn't seem worth it.

"Sam, we have to get down to ..."

"... business." I blew on my coffee, burned myself with another taste. "You know, I always used to hear that a lot at work too. I used to just laugh at Triandos behind his back when he said that."

My lack of ambition was a subject Clare and I had argued over a lot. I ended every argument by making fun of myself. She could always see right through me. She made me feel naked, but it was a good naked, acceptable and even stimulating in our own

little private place.

Seven months after we met, I quit college after my junior year to follow blindly after Clare, showing up at her apartment door trailing clouds of glory. We were in so much heat we hardly had the focus to scrabble together a little wedding ceremony by the end of the summer. It was a tiny little event, but I wanted my mother to see it before she died. Clare's parents were there, and we each had a few college friends. My mother had suffered a stroke during my last semester of college, and I knew she was at the beginning of her last passage. At least she lived to see Clare pregnant, the two of us bound together like no two souls ever before, and she had to know that part of her would live forever in us.

It turned out that I wasn't that suited for making a living, but there was one thing I could do: I could make Clare laugh. I thought I had found my life's work. Kate came along and proved that I was right. But it had been a long time since Clare thought my jokes were funny. Over the past few years, our lovemaking had fallen off, but I supposed that happened to everybody, and I thought at least it was happening to us together. What about the fact that she hadn't let me touch her in six months? What did I do about that? Here's what I did. I closed my eyes, anesthetized myself for her.

"We don't have to talk, Sam, if you don't want to." The trace of pity in her eyes was humiliating. "I left some clothes, pictures, knickknacks, little things. I can just go upstairs and get them now and get it over with. We can talk through lawyers, if that's what you want."

"No, no lawyers. Take what you want. I'll help you."

I followed her to the bedroom. She stopped in front of our wedding picture framed above the bureau. I didn't expect her to take it, and she didn't. I did not let her take every picture of young Kate.

"I have a few empty boxes in the trunk of my car."

"I'll get them for you."

She gathered up a few pictures, some clothes she had forgotten, combs, brushes, a makeup mirror, a little real estate plaque she had won and hung on the bedroom wall, her jewelry, the rest of her shoes. I just stood there as she erased herself from my life. After she had stripped every trace of herself from the room, she turned and held my eyes.

"I shouldn't wear these any more."

She pulled off her wedding and engagement rings and held them out to me in the palm of her hand. I froze. She took my hand and tried to close it around the rings, but my fingers went numb and would not move. She caught the rings and gently laid them on the top of the bureau.

Outside, she thanked me, then turned away quickly to open the car door.

"You can't mean this, Clare. You can't want us to end."

"It's already ended, Sam."

It was the same green-eyed look I had fallen in love with, but there was nothing but pity in those eyes now. That kind of look lasts only so long until it turns into disgust. I turned away to get out of her sight quickly. I turned back. If she could really see how much I loved her, she would understand. My hands were on the sill of her car window. She did have sufficient pity not to start the car and drag me down the street.

I heard the phone ring inside the house.

"We need to talk about Kate." I took my hands off the car. "You are leaving both of us, me and her."

"We'll talk about all that." No pity now, she was staring straight ahead through the windshield. The whole neighborhood was glowing cold white under the searing sun.

"I mean it. I want Kate."

24

Chapter 3

Principal Freeland turns away and walks into the gym, closing the door behind him. The only thing I can hear then is the sound of my own breathing. The next thing I know I'm sitting on a metal chair at the very back row of the gym trying to pull my blouse together, but my hands are much too shaky. Lucky is sitting next to me.

"What ...?"

"Shhhh! Just be quiet, please."

The door clangs open and one of the teachers drags Johnson by the hand into the gym.

"No, no, Mrs. Whitson." Principal Freeland is suddenly directing things from the stage in his amplified voice. "Randy Johnson, we're glad to welcome you to our assembly!" Mr. Freeland is a new principal who suddenly appeared at the school a few weeks ago. He has a big jaw and a wide set of teeth that he likes everyone to see, but he isn't really smiling. He shows his teeth to Johnson all the way from the podium. "Welcome, Randy. Mr. Whitson, bring Randy Johnson up front here, to the front row. Randy, we want you to know that you are very welcome here. We'll make room."

Lucky leans toward me.

"What did he do to you?"

I can't answer.

"Somebody should kick his ass. He doesn't belong in school

with regular people."

There might be some asbestos in the building, Freeland announces. Starting in January, we are going to have all of our classes in trailers.

"I want you to know that there is no proof of danger now. We've had the air tested and there is no asbestos in the air right now. But the county is growing, and Glenwood Junior High may have to expand anyway to avoid being overcrowded in the very near future. Beginning in January, county engineers will come in and study the building, take apart the heating and cooling system, look at the plumbing and electrical wiring and all the other systems.

"So I have developed a plan. I located some trailers and I'm having them brought here. I've decided to put the trailers on the soccer field next to the woods. We'll have classes in the trailers beginning next semester, and maybe sooner. It's for your own safety.

"I want to be extra careful with every student's health. A letter went out to each of your parents yesterday, and we will be giving a copy to each of you today."

I'm still shaking. Lucky leans in close. As soon as I feel a touch, my hand goes up and hits his face.

"Kate, it's me."

He leans over and buttons up my shirt like it's the most natural thing in the world to do.

"They don't see anything," I say. "They don't see me. They don't see Johnson either. He's sitting in the front row and they don't even see that he's all beat up."

"They see what they want to see. All Freeland wants to see right now is a bunch of scared kids."

Lucky walks with me in the crowd returning from the assembly.

"Kate, come with me to the woods after school."

"To get wasted?"

"I want to show you something."

"Animal, vegetable or penis?" I'm just giving him a hard time. The thing is, he has no idea how hot he is. He has no idea that I'd go anywhere in the world with him.

"Remember the other day, when you asked what happened to me?"

"You never told me."

"It's hard to tell. I want to show you."

My English teacher, Ms. Nesbitt, notices I'm a mess and takes me out into the hall. Diane thinks Nesbitt is skewed. Sometimes it's hard to tell if Ms. Nesbitt is really looking at you. I can't figure out if she's cool or not.

"What happened to you, Kate?"

"Nothing. I ... tripped outside the gym."

Just then, Principal Freeland struts by.

"Problem?" He slows his pace just a bit, his eyebrows raised. Freeland's pale blue eyes pin me down.

"I'm okay."

Ms. Nesbitt raises her arched red eyebrows even higher but says nothing. Freeland dips his head and goes on by.

"Do you want to go home, Kate?" Ms. Nesbitt is not buying my story.

"No."

"This didn't happen to you at home, did it?"

"No. But there's nobody there. At home, I mean. I mean now."

"I never saw anybody's shirt get ripped at the collar like that by tripping in the grass."

"Please," I beg. Her stare is a little off center, like a dog who's trying to figure out what you're saying. "Please, can you just send Diane out for a sec?"

Diane helps me fix my blouse with a paperclip. I tell Diane what Johnson did.

"Let's go home. I'll go with you."

"I really want to stay, Diane."

"Then you definitely need a lavatory break. A little makeup and a hair brush."

"Oh. Forget it. What do I care?"

"Come on, Kate," she says, rolling her eyes at the crowd of kids in the hallway. "If you start to look like a mess, they'll start picking on you too. They're predators, going after the weak ones. Don't be a straggler."

It's true. The kids rag on whoever they think is the weakest link. Until last summer when I found out I didn't really have a family, I never thought I'd have to worry about that. Diane clicks her tongue as she arranges my clothes and hair with quick smooth hands like a mother. She's so intent she doesn't need to talk. For a minute.

"You know what Lucky said about the asbestos, the asbestos they're practically tearing the school down for? He says there never has been any asbestos in the building."

"Oh yeah? How would he know?"

"Hey, I'm just telling you what I hear. You're the one who swaps secrets with him in the woods."

"Maybe I'll find out. When I go down there with him this afternoon."

"Oh, you tramp! You lucky tramp! You must tell all, you know. Now I really must get you beautified." As we walk out of the lavatory door, she's worried again about me being easy prey in the halls: "Repeat after me. Must not be mussed. Must remember outcome of fight. Must remember knee in balls."

"Diane, you are so great."

"Of course."

I meet Lucky at the side door of the school and we walk across the soccer field. Nobody is out there practicing yet. We push through the brush at the edge of the field, mostly Queen Anne's lace gone all white and furry at the top. We pick our way through a thicket of barberry bushes showing off thousands of their tiny red leaves. Then the trail slants downhill, and the huge trees that crowd the edge of the trail make us feel small. Down at our level, weeds and vines and honeysuckle wrestle themselves into huge tangles. Ferns curl out between black rocks.

Lucky's eyes take in everything in the woods. For a while a stream runs next to the path. So many red and yellow leaves float on its surface you can see only a couple of sparkles of water in between. Then the stream curves and crosses the path, running under a wooden bridge. Lucky stops at the bridge and stares at the water ten feet below.

"What?"

He lowers himself all the way down the dirt bank, grabbing roots to slow himself down, and doesn't stop until just before his feet go in the stream. Then he waves for me to follow. Fine roots hang straight down from the banks like long hair brushing our faces. There is no flat space for walking at the edge of the stream, so for a while we hop rocks. Lucky doesn't talk. With his head shaved, he looks like some kind of Iroquois hunter, the sun flickering off the bare sides of his head as he leads me forward. Then he climbs out of the stream and goes up a hill covered with prickly bushes and gets onto a new path, a narrow red dirt path under the shade of high trees. There's no sound but the rustling of the leaves and the soft padding noises of our sneakers on the dirt.

Lucky climbs a small hill up ahead and stops. The woods suddenly end just at the bottom of the hill, and down below there is a little valley stretching across in front of us. A narrow white road runs through the valley. There are only a couple of houses on either side of the road. We are staring right into the back yard of one of them.

It's some kind of ranch-shaped thing with walls made out to look like it's a log cabin. Every side of the house that we can see has some kind of porch or deck attached to it, all made out of the same greenish wood. This house has a split rail fence

29

around the back yard. Another fence, made out of small squares of metal wire, is nailed inside the split rail fence. Either one of these fences might look okay by itself.

We sit at the edge of the woods looking down over this scene.

"Somebody ought to do something about that Johnson," he says.

"Let's not talk about him. You said you would tell me the stuff that happened to you."

He still hesitates. Come on, how bad could it be?

"I'm going to be pissed if all we're going to do is sit here and stare at the backyard of some house."

"Last summer, right after my father left, I used to drink in the woods, go to the trail every night and skate and drink until I was sick. Rat used to get the stuff for me. He's just pissed that I don't do it any more."

"Why did you stop?"

"Duh, Kate. It's stupid, puking your guts out night after night."

"So you're smarter than me?"

"That's not what I mean. After my father finally moved out, I tore up the house. My mother called the cops on me, and they actually took me to court and all that."

"That really sucks."

"Well, I did tear up my mother's house. At least the family room. This log cabin," he points down the hill, "is my father's new house. It's about three miles away by road, but my mother doesn't know you can cut through the woods and get here in fifteen minutes."

There are decorations all over the house, all over the decks and in the yard – trellises, flower boxes, bird feeders, benches, wind chimes, a little propeller on a pole. There are two doghouses.

"Are we going there now?"

"Um, something else a little funny. I'll be right back." He looks back. "Really, don't come down the hill yet."

He runs down the hill and vaults over the fence. Two huge dogs come running out of their houses, barking like crazy. Lucky puts his arms out and they both jump on him at the same time and knock him flat on his back. They try to lick his face, and he rolls around on the ground. Finally he stands up.

I wait for him go to the back door, but instead he goes over to one of the birdhouses. It's on a high pole, one of those apartment birdhouses with six or eight little bird holes. Lucky goes around behind and puts his arm into like the attic of the birdhouse. He pulls something heavy out and looks at the back door of the house, but then he turns around and walks back toward the woods. The dogs follow him to the fence.

I can see before he even gets over the fence that it's a gun, some kind of huge, shiny, chrome gun.

"What are you doing?" I yell. Lucky just puts it in his waistband and chugs up the hill.

"What are you doing? What the hell?"

"I'm not going to shoot anything." He reaches the top. "Something strange. Just wait."

We sit down and watch the house. Then a little brown Nissan comes across on the road in front of the house, leaving a trail of white dust behind it. It pulls into the driveway of the house and stops. A woman steps out. She is pretty tall and wearing tight jeans, and her reddish brown hair is pulled up and pinned in a loose bun. Lucky doesn't make a move, even after she reaches the back deck, pets the dogs, gets out her keys, opens the door and goes in.

By this time it's chilly. The last half of the red sun is sinking down into the trees on the other side of the valley.

"That wasn't my father."

"No kidding. Who is she?"

"Rudi, my father's girlfriend."

It's getting colder. Nobody says anything. Lucky is staring straight down at the house.

A black pickup truck with a ladder on top shoots down the road with an even higher cloud of dust. It turns in and skitters to a crunchy stop in the driveway.

"Hold your ears," Lucky shouts.

"What?"

"Do it."

As soon as a man gets out, Lucky picks up his gun and shoots it straight up in the air. The shot rings hard in my ears. Bad-smelling smoke is all around us. By the time I look up, the man is halfway back through the yard, coming towards us. Swatting at the dogs, he gets to the back fence and hops it like a deer. He starts up the hill toward us.

He has Lucky's eyes, but his hair is more of a reddish brown with some grey in it. You can see that he once tried to dye it. But he's great looking, if you like weatherbeaten faces.

"This your girlfriend?"

"Nah. This is Kate."

"Howdy, Kate. How do you like our wireless communication system?"

He has a wide, warm smile.

"Hi." I just can't help but smile back at this guy.

"Yeah. I'm always losing those cell phones. But I'd recognize the sound of that .357 anywhere."

"I can't come to your house any more," Lucky interrupts.

"What the hell? What the hell is your mother up to now? Sorry, honey." He glances at me.

"Now I have to report to probation every week."

"What?" He looks at Lucky. "Oh shit! Shit, no! What happened?"

"She came to pick me up here last week. She caught me and Rudi smoking pot."

"And she called her lawyer? Without calling me? That's her

way of setting things straight?"

"I'm not supposed to come here any more at all." Lucky seems really bitter.

"We'll work our way out of this. You're still working with me on Saturdays, right?"

"I can go, but I have to stay on the site. Mom will drop me off at the site. And she has to pick me up at the site. She doesn't want me coming to your house."

"Come on in the house right now."

"No."

Lucky's father stretches himself up. "You shouldn't be smoking that pot, but Jesus, can't she give a kid a break?" He turns away and stares at the sun sinking low and the twilight creeping slowly into the valley. You don't know how quiet the woods are until you stop talking.

"Your mother's starting to talk like she hates me. A long time ago, she used to think there was some kind of genius in me. I guess I fooled her for a while. Maybe that's why she's so mad now, because I fooled her for so long."

"If she catches me coming in, I'll never be allowed to see you again."

"Oh well, son. Don't worry so much. Nothing's ever final in this kind of thing. We'll work on it. I'll talk to Rudi."

"Here's the gun back."

Lucky walks with me all the way through the woods and back to my house.

"What's the story with Rudi?"

"My father's new girlfriend. She lives with him in the house."

"Do you like her?"

"No. I hate her. But she did give me pot. That was cool."

Chapter 4

We don't use tooth and claw to fight for our offspring any more, but still we hunch in a circle and stare. We had been called in to a meeting in Principal Freeland's office, I assumed to talk about what kind of punishment Johnson would get for attacking Kate, or at least to talk about getting him out of Kate's class.

"Excuse me, Principal Freeland. This meeting is illegal under federal law."

The woman with the bright red lipstick, I found out, was that kid Johnson's lawyer. Mindy Faye had a way of pretending to smile that resulted in her baring her teeth a lot. She wore leather sandals and a long shapeless floral dress. Mindy was tall, broad-shouldered and plump, but she talked in an insinuating, whining, little-girl voice.

"We're just having a friendly little meeting here." Principal Freeland was trying to be folksy, but he wasn't the folksy type. Freeland was fifty-ish, with thick, blonde, graying hair, a big square jaw, steel-rimmed glasses and a wide, toothy politician's smile. Freeland seemed like he was accustomed to plowing over the opposition. Folksy didn't fit him too well.

"It doesn't matter what you call it. Federal regulations prohibit any meeting at which Randy Johnson's diagnosis, or any other confidential material in his file, may be disclosed. It is a violation of federal law to discuss any part of the plan with any person other than the parent, the parent's attorney, the Paid

Independent Service Provider, or a school administrator who can demonstrate and articulate a specific need to know."

"All I want to know is, what are the chances he'll try it again?" I said.

"That would be prognosis. We can't talk about diagnosis or prognosis."

"You can't tell us ...?" I looked at Kate. She looked so unhappy, almost like she was the one who had done something wrong.

"Fine," I said quickly. "Let's talk about the 'Paid Independent Service Provider.' I'm guessing she is the same person the kids call the 'guard.' How much does she get paid for not showing up and not protecting my daughter from this boy?"

"It is a violation of federal regulations," Mindy repeated, "to discuss the plan at any meeting at which non-authorized persons are present."

I looked at Freeland. He looked back blankly. He didn't look like he cared about either Mindy Faye or me. He looked like he was just trying to find a way to make this trivial and irritating matter go away.

"Fine," I said. "We'll just go to the police."

I stood up to go.

Freeland jerked up in his chair and slapped his hand down on his desk.

"No!"

Everybody froze.

"Mrs. Johnson," Freeland pointedly ignored the lawyer and focused his piercing blue eyes directly on Randy Johnson's mother. "Mr. Alexander has every right to call the police, but I don't think any of us here really wants him to do that."

"No." She was almost whimpering.

"So this meeting can be an official, federal Periodic Plan Review Team Meeting, or it can be – and I suggest that we make it be – some other kind of meeting." I could tell Freeland was used to getting his way. "So this can be just an informal meeting between two parents, two children, the teacher and the principal."

"Any meeting discussing, or purporting to discuss, the behavior of the challenged individual constitutes a PPRTM, and all of the protections of the PPRTM apply." Mindy Faye's patronizing smile was more phony even than Freeland's. "You can't get around the requirements of the PPRTM by calling it something else." She looked at each of us in turn, showing her teeth.

"Kate, let's go. I should have just called the police."

"Mr. Alexander, sit down." Freeland's voice again resonated with sudden power. He turned to Mindy Faye. "I'm convening this meeting right now. It's just an informal meeting, not a PPRTM. Anybody in this room who wants to participate can participate. Anybody who wants to leave may leave."

I sat down. The Johnson kid was just across the semicircle from me. He had pulled his chair back and away from his mother. His legs were crossed and he was wiggling one foot like crazy while picking at a scab. His mother was trying to pull his hands down from his face.

Mindy Faye suddenly pushed herself into the middle of the circle and bent down to face Johnson, giving me a close-up view of her enormous rear end. Johnson immediately grabbed for her hair. Mindy caught Johnson's wrist with one hand, but then Johnson reached out for her face with his other hand. Fighting him off, she dropped all her notes on the floor.

"Randy," Mindy ignored the mess on the floor and began pretending to talk to Johnson. She kept it up, in a maudlin little girl's voice, even as their hand-to-hand combat intensified. Kate shrank back in her chair. Johnson, who had been just sitting there spacing out during all of the first part of the meeting, had a look of grim determination on his face, as if his sole aim in life was to get his fingers in Mindy's frowzy, yellow-grey hair. All the while, Mindy talked only to him. The rest of us just sat there, too embarrassed to admit we could hear.

"We're going to have a meeting, Randy. But it won't be an official PPRTM, understand? You have a right to a PPRTM, and I'm going to insist on one within the next thirty days. You understand, right? But this is just a regular school meeting right now. But we won't do it unless I have your permission. Do I have your permission?"

Johnson didn't seem to have anything on his mind but getting his hands in Mindy's hair.

"No, no, Randy. I know you like me. I like you too, Randy, but you can't grab my hair. I'll give you a hug later. Right now I need to know if it's okay with you if we have this meeting right now to talk about you, just informally. And we'll have the official PPRTM later."

She was pretty quick with her own hands, and soon the spark went out of his eyes and he let his wrists hang limp in Mindy's grasp. Then he went limp all over and allowed Mindy to push him back into a slumped-over position on his chair.

"My client has given his permission for us to proceed with the meeting," she informed us.

Johnson suddenly stood up on wobbly knees and staggered across towards Kate. Kate leaned way back in her chair and put up one foot to kick out at him, and he backed off. Mindy got between him and Kate, forcing him to back off and sit down. Then she squatted down on the floor and held another embarrassing one-way conversation with her client.

"Let's get on with the meeting," Freeland commanded.

"I just want to know what will be done to make sure Kate is not attacked again," I said.

"Kate, dear," Mindy, still squatting on the floor, twisted back to address Kate. "We understand that it must have felt like an attack, but ..."

"It was an attack."

"You must understand that people like Randy Johnson are so often misunderstood. Their methods of communication are often unusual, and sometimes frightening."

"He ripped my blouse." Kate was sobbing. "He grabbed me by the hair. He scratched me everywhere. He slammed my head against the wall."

"Randy Johnson is a very clumsy child, Kate. We can't expect ..."

"Dad!" Kate hissed at me. "Are you going to let them say this? Dad?"

I jumped up and stamped my foot in the middle of the circle like some sort of cave man fighting off poisonous snakes.

"Cut the crap! He did it! I know it! Tell me how you're going to stop him, or I'm going to the police right now."

Freeland stared at me from behind his steel glasses. I expected everyone else to regroup around Freeland and circle in on me for the kill, but Mindy and Freeland hated each other too much to join forces against me. The silence dragged on. Finally, Johnson's mother shouted out.

"Oh, God!"

Everyone followed Mrs. Johnson's eyes to Kate. Kate had pulled her shirt up and her bra down far enough for everyone to see three angry red lines scratched across her chest. I jumped toward Johnson, then stopped myself.

"Are you satisfied?" I yelled. Everyone else was looking down at the floor. Except Johnson, who was staring at Kate's breasts.

"No apologies for doubting her?" I said. "Nobody has anything to say?"

I pulled Kate up by the hand and we were out of that circle, out of that room. I did make her stop and pull her clothes together. I put my hand on her shoulder and slowed her down as we walked through the outer office, down the halls and out the door. People looked away. We stopped and stood together outside on the sidewalk.

"I think we're pretty much on our own in dealing with this guy, Kate. What do you want me to do? I'd punch his lights out, but I'm trying to be an adult here."

She didn't answer.

The heavy steel door clanked open behind us. Principal Freeland came out alone. Kate stood facing him. Freeland made eye contact with each of us and gave us a resigned look like there was nothing he could do. I had a strange feeling that he was glad there was nothing he could do. I knew the main thing he wanted was that nobody call the police.

"They admit he did it," he said. "Now they're blaming the school for what he did. There's a company we pay $45,000 a year to send a personal aide in every day just to watch him. The company has promised that, from now on, the aide will actually be there to watch him every day.

"Kate never has to sit next to him, never. And if there is a day when both the aide and the substitute aide fail to show, Kate is excused from class, and Mr. Folsom will make some arrangements to tutor her personally for that lesson."

"What happens to that kid?" I asked.

Freeland squinted at me. "As I said, Johnson gets supervised more closely."

"What happens when we move to the trailers?" Kate suddenly piped in.

I hadn't heard anything about trailers. Freeland stepped back and put both hands on his hips.

"What's this about trailers?" I said.

Freeland's voice dropped. "Mr. Alexander, I have a concern about asbestos. Some people say it's too much of a concern. I need to close the building for a while to check out if there's asbestos in the building."

"There's no asbestos in the building." Kate was staring right at Freeland with her arms folded. If you looked hard, you could still see the beginning of one of the red scratch marks at the collar of her shirt.

"Most people involved do think that there's no immediate danger from asbestos." Freeland was suddenly cagey.

"There's no asbestos." Kate rolled her eyes. "Lucky told me."

"As I told the parents in a letter which you should be receiving today," Freeland looked me right in the eyes, "even the experts aren't certain. But you know teenagers. They're all experts about things they know nothing about."

I had some experience with people who look you right in the eyes. Sometimes, when people look you right in the eyes, they are lying to you. I couldn't shake the feeling that this was one of those times.

"What are you doing?"

Triandos's voice startled me.

"Um, looking at my calendar."

"From last year?"

It was true. It was my monthly daybook, where I used to write down all the things we had done each weekend – just to remind myself why I went to work every day. I had piled up three or four old calendars from past years. "Kate's Eighth Grade Assembly" was written on the calendar for a Friday night exactly a year ago. I wish I had known then that this was the last thing Clare and I would ever do together.

"I was just, um, checking on something."

"Maybe you'd be better off looking at this year's calendar and working on those bids today. Your evaluations of those bids are due next week, and you've been dragging your feet."

"Oh. Next week. I hadn't realized that."

"Now you do." He turned to go. Triandos was a tolerant boss. I got away with a lot because I did at least a little bit of work every day, but he knew I laughed about the job behind his back. It wouldn't have mattered to me last year that he talked to me like this, but now it did.

"Boss? It's not just laziness. I've been trying to retrace some things in my life since Clare moved out. I can't explain it. I won't do it on work time."

"Fair enough." He looked me in the eyes. "I'm sure it's awful. Just try to focus on work while you're here."

My phone rang just then, and my heart jumped with a premonition that it was Clare. It was. "Clare. Wait a second." I looked at Triandos, and he turned and went out.

"I'll be over in your office in a minute, boss."

"Take your time."

"How are you, Sam?" The sound of Clare's voice on the phone slid over my frazzled nerves like warm honey.

"How are you, Clare?"

"We have so many things to settle, Sam."

"I keep thinking you're not really so sure. I know you've ... done some things. But nothing's final. Don't we want to wait a while, to see how things work out?"

"I am sure of what I want, Sam. We do have to talk business, Sam, if we don't want to involve lawyers."

"You mean, date of separation and all that?"

"That date's already happened, Sam."

"Oh. Oh. Yeah. Of course."

"We need to decide how we're going to do custody, Sam, and how we're going to divide up things."

"I told you I want Kate."

Clare was in some kind of fantasy real estate dream world, completely infatuated with Anton and living a life with him that didn't leave room for Kate. And even before Anton, there had always been in our marriage a tiny, nagging undercurrent of Clare's disappointment with Kate. Was it because there was too much of me in her? I could never talk about Kate's side of things without being accused of criticizing Clare.

41

"And I don't want to sell the house until she's out of high school," I added. "That's all I want. You can have all the rest."

"We can't freeze everything for that long. And if you're getting the house for four years, I want a reasonable share of your pension. But we'd be fools to cash in the pension this early. I need something to live on now, Sam."

Live on Anton, I thought. You're doing a fine job of it already. But I didn't say this. This would end the conversation right away. And I couldn't stand for all my conversations with her to be forever over.

"Maybe we can get it over quick, Sam. Maybe you can keep the whole house, pension, everything, and you could give me Alexander's Woods."

"The woods? Those are mine. It's the only thing I got when Mom died."

"You're taking everything else."

I knew I had some kind of special rights to those woods, even in a divorce, since I inherited them after we were married; but that wasn't the reason I couldn't let them go.

"I'm not taking everything else." My voice sounded weak even to me. "You can have the house after Kate finishes high school."

"You're going around in circles. If we give this to the lawyers to fight it out, they'll take most of it themselves. You know that."

"How can you expect me," I knew I shouldn't say this even as I was saying it, "to let you and Anton build your own house, on my Mom's property, and then have to drive by there myself every day and see that?"

"Oh. I see you refuse to be rational. It will just get worse for you, Sam, if we don't reach an agreement soon to put this thing behind us. Goodbye."

Clare was raised in a tiny house on a magnificent but decaying street in Kinston, where the Carolina landed gentry once built their Victorian city homes. I was raised on a non-working farm ten miles outside of Glenwood. Neither of us ever felt at home in suburban Glenwood, and we always planned to sell the little house with the carport and build a real house right in Alexander's Woods. I knew that it made no sense to hold on to those woods any more. Hanging onto those woods was probably just postponing the day when I'd be able to live by the normal rules of the mind.

Chapter 5

Glenwood is a pretty old suburb. My Dad went to the same school I do now, in the same buildings. On a hot day, you can smell the decades of layers of shellac on the floor. You're not supposed to open the old windows any more because there's now an air conditioning system. When it doesn't work, Ms. Nesbitt will ask two or three of the stronger boys to pry the windows open.

There are no screens, and all kinds of things fly in. Every time a yellow jacket buzzes in, Ms. Nesbitt assigns someone to kill it. Then the deceased's time and date of death is written down, and the corpse is taped into a copybook which she calls the Book of the Dead.

Ms. Nesbitt is tall and skinny, with curly red hair that she usually pulls back with a blue plastic clip. When she doesn't, it sticks out from her head like springs. She tilts her head a little to the side when she's listening, like a dog. She teaches Advanced English class, where we are supposed to be creative. You can say anything you want in her class.

"I'm sick of being taught in trailers." It's so great that this has nothing to do with Hamlet, that we were talking about two seconds ago, and Nesbitt doesn't mind. Diane can get Nesbitt to talk about anything. "I was taught in trailers in the second, third and fourth grade."

"I was in a trailer almost every year in elementary school," somebody else says.

"Maybe we should write letters of protest to the County Council," Ms. Nesbitt suggests. "That's who really controls whatever happens here."

"They're tearing the whole school down," I say. "Everybody knows it. Nobody can stop it. Don't make us write letters too."

"Yeah, you're just making it worse," Lucky says.

Ms. Nesbitt puts a hand on her hip.

"Don't you care about how other people feel?" Johnny Gott, who once wore a giant plastic penis to a girl's party, says this. "If they set up the trailers on the soccer field, where will we practice?"

"Tomorrow," Ms. Nesbitt declares, "we will hold a memorial service for the dead soccer field. It will start at the usual time for this class." She looks up at the ceiling like God is telling her this. "This will be a non-denominational, non-sectarian service for a soccer season murdered by progress. No crucifixes, Stars of David, prayer wheels or statues of Buddha allowed. We will each mourn in our creative way the death of the life that took place out there on that field every day."

Mostly, the boys wear their oversize T-shirts and the girls wear lots of jewelry. We are supposed to wrap ourselves in black crepe paper and slowly walk around the track that runs around the soccer field. Ms. Nesbitt takes the lead with her head bowed.

That's all there is to it. Ms. Nesbitt doesn't even care if kids wear earbuds and listen to music. The grass inside the track is wet and shiny from the dew. There are large muddy spots in the middle, from soccer practices. A lot of kids, like Johnny Gott, and even Diane, do like soccer, and I don't get why the field's being torn down when there isn't really even any asbestos. We only go around the track once, then Ms. Nesbitt leads the procession across the field and back toward the school, circling around the muddy spots. Ms. Nesbitt is definitely crazy, but this place would be so boring without her.

Mr. Freeland comes walking out of the back door of the school, but Ms. Nesbitt walks right by, nodding like it's part of the deal. Freeland is quiet, but his eyes move fast. He's so pissed off it makes the whole scene worth it. He follows us back into the classroom.

Ms. Nesbitt forces one of the kids to tell him what just happened.

"I see," Freeland says. "You're not happy you'll be in trailers again." I know Freeland really couldn't care less. If I asked Lucky, he'd say, of course it's nothing to Freeland. He won't be in a trailer. He doesn't play soccer.

Ms. Nesbitt just stands there with one hand on her hip staring at Freeland like he's a genius. Mr. Freeland clears his throat, waits. He thinks Ms. Nesbitt is going to say something, but we all know she isn't.

"Ms. Nesbitt is a very open-minded teacher, and she's allowed the class to express their feelings creatively, and I commend her for that. But I'm responsible for this school, and we have our image in the community to consider. And we have rules about special events. Requirements for parental permission slips, for one thing. Ms. Nesbitt and I will discuss this later."

"Can't we have more classes outside – maybe in the soccer stands before they're all torn down?" Lucky yells this out at Mr. Freeland like he's just another guy on a construction site or something.

"I don't think that would be a good idea. The foundations for the trailers are coming in soon, and ..."

"People say there's no asbestos in the building, so we don't need trailers."

The kids turn around and look at Lucky now.

"People say a lot of things. One of the skills every student should learn is critical thinking."

"Where is the asbestos? My father's a contractor. He worked

on the heating system, and ..."

"Okay. Hold it. Hold it." Mr Freeland holds up his hand. "I can't debate this engineering issue now."

"Okay, sir. But what is your opinion about outdoor classes?" Mr. Freeland's face is getting red. "If we were outdoors more, we wouldn't be around this dangerous asbestos so much. And we wouldn't, you know, be thinking and talking about asbestos all the time."

I can tell he hates Lucky. He doesn't like hard questions, and he just wants to get out of the room. I'm afraid of what he might do now.

"On second thought, it seems like a pretty simple request to me. Some outdoor English classes over the next few days. Why not? I don't see how it can really do any harm."

Lucky follows me down the corridor after the class.

"So, what do you think?"

"I think you two – you and Diane – are awesome."

"No, I mean about what I showed you in the woods the other day."

"Your Dad? I think he's really cool."

"He is, isn't he? I can't see him, you know, officially. But I still see him more than I actually see my Mom. She works all the time."

"I'd sneak over there too if I were you, Lucky. I would."

"Do you want to see something else?"

"You mean more weird stuff."

"Another thing nobody knows about. Meet me here after school."

Lucky's the only boy from that day I got drunk in the woods who ever talked to me again. His family is more of a mess than mine, but he laughs about it. I wish I could be so cool about it like that.

Lucky has to report to Mr. Freeland's office right after school, so I take my time in the hall, cramming stuff in and pulling stuff out of my locker. I'm still in a dreamy mood, imagining Lucky and I walking in the woods alone. I'm not paying attention to anything else, but then I look up and see Johnson limping down the corridor towards me. He's alone and without his guard.

He tries to say something to two girls coming the other way, but they just giggle and walk right by like they don't even see him. Then he turns and heads right for me.

"Kate." His voice is soft, and he stalks over to me so slowly you can hardly notice his limp. "Wait."

He has a really sad look on his face, like he's going to apologize. My heart is pounding like it knows I should run, but everybody at the meeting said he might have misunderstood.

"No touch!" I shout. "No touching, Randy. No touching. Right?"

I know he's stupid, and I must be too, because I wait too long for an answer that doesn't come – until he smashes into me and slams me against the lockers. He's got me pinned against the wall. His medication smell turns my stomach. He's groaning like a pig and pushing his slobbery face toward mine, but I turn my head. I feel his hands under my sweater. I scream out, but nobody comes. He backs away a little, his one hand still gripping my breast like a claw, and I look down to see what he's doing. He's trying to unbuckle his belt with the other hand. I guess I've taught him how to rape.

My hands are like jelly and just as spastic as his, but I'm jamming my fingers between his hand and the belt and trying to dig my nails into his skin. If that buckle opens, he's going to pump his filth into me and turn me into a dirty animal like him. I don't want to keep on living if that happens. I'm biting him on the arm so hard he takes his hand off my breast. He forgets to keep me pinned against the lockers. He's pushing one hand into my face and still trying to get the buckle open. He can't do it. I push him back and get enough room.

Chapter 6 ✍

Lucky's given up waiting for me and is across the school lawn and getting into a car before I catch up. I don't tell him anything. His stepfather, Ralph, drives us to a pathetic little building in an industrial park. Lucky has to go in there and let a fat man watch him pee in a cup.

"I just wanted you to see that," he says later.

"What's so weird about that? You're on probation."

He's thinking this is so weird, and it isn't. Even his stepfather is pretty nice, though it must be so boring to hear him talk all day about what Lucky's mother would approve. I imagine Lucky meeting my own mother, with her beautiful cheekbones and her smart suit, and I wonder if he'd be able to tell right away that she is really a witch who hates me. I'm wondering what he would think about me if he knew that moron Johnson groped me again.

I burn the pizza trying to make dinner for Dad after he comes home, so he goes in the dining room right away with a whole pile of folders from his work and starts punching on a calculator and writing on papers. He used to be so funny before Mom did this to him. My friends loved him. Mom laughed too and said he wasn't normal. Maybe she felt she had to leave so I could grow up normal myself. What chance is there of that?

"I've never seen you work with a calculator before."

"How are you doing, Kate?" He spreads the fingers of his

hands and holds them out and stares at the papers like they might jump up at him. Does a normal person work in the dark with a tiny spotlight that shines on only one page at a time?

"Oh. I'm doing utterly fantastic, Dad."

"That's good."

He looks back at his papers, stares at the wall, looks down. Then he stares at the wall again. I pull a chair up to the corner of the table, but he doesn't look up. He doesn't say anything more, and he doesn't do anything with his papers either. So, if he's bad off, how bad off am I just sitting and watching him?

"Sorry about the pizza. Maybe I can make you some more coffee?"

"That's nice, Kate. Uh, no thanks."

"Are you sad about Mom leaving, Dad?"

He looks past me at the wall.

"Because I'm not."

"Sorry, Kate," he says. "I'm ... I'm ..." He forgets that we're talking.

So, here's my mistake, thinking that I still exist as far as he is concerned. He's breathing real slow and deep, like he's meditating, but his mouth is clamped shut like he's in pain. It's like he's in a coma. I just want to slap him awake.

"Johnson hit me again today."

"That's nice, Kate."

A long time later he comes out of his trance, but he just looks down at his papers again and starts writing.

"Dad?"

The only light is from his tiny desk lamp making a sharp little circle on the table. I'm invisible here in the dark. This is too much like the dream I have every night. I cross into the living room and stare out the front window at the white moon stealing up over the houses across the street. It's hard to believe the moon is as great a goal as Mr. Folsom makes it out to be. It might be beautiful, but it's almost as cold as the deep black space behind around me.

"Teach me to skate."

Out on the trail, one of Lucky's friends has already crashed, dropping his flashlight – but then he pops up suddenly, cursing and laughing. Lucky does put his arm around my waist, but the whole deal is much more tippy than I expected and I'm grabbing onto him and my legs are lurching back and forth. Not the romantic scene I hoped for, but he really is showing me how to skate. He says if I step on and off the skateboard every time I get going too fast, I might make it to the bottom.

"Try it yourself now." He lets me go, but I hold tight to his hand, almost falling into him when the skateboard pulls away.

"Where?"

He points down the trail.

"You're kidding."

He isn't. I let go of his hand and wobble forward, my wheels rumbling. I can feel my skateboard's wheels moving on the hard surface, but it's so dark I can't really see anything below my knees. Right away I'm going too fast. If I put my foot on the ground now I'll do a split. I might as well try for a miracle. The cold air is rushing against my face. I'm going too fast to make the first turn, but I try it anyway, fantasizing about floating magically in and out of the moon shadows.

The skateboard stops dead and slams me into a bank, the earth punching me hard. My body's like in a straightjacket of pain and I can't take in any air. I know I'm dying, and it's so painful I just want it to be over. I can hear Lucky and the other guys run up. They can talk, so I know they can breathe, and I am so jealous of that. Lucky pulls me out of the bushes and helps me stand up, my mouth open and gasping for air that won't come.

"Kate, you'll be fine." Lucky doesn't know I can't breathe, and I can't tell him, because I can't talk. "You just got the wind knocked out of you. You'll be okay soon. Just hang on."

Just like Lucky says, my chest begins to let me take in little

it. Maybe the "almost" is the important part. Maybe Mr. Folsom is trying to say you should find something real between yourself and the blackness and then just go for it.

I look at Dad with his head down, working on his papers. The cold quiet coming off of him fills that room like an invisible poison gas, and it starts to creep up around my ankles and fill up this room too. It's really simple. I have to run for my life. Dad is so out of it I don't need to sneak out. I even open the hallway closet to pick up my coat.

Outside, the street is empty. The moon is etched with soft white mountains. The houses are just dark shapes closed against all those who don't belong in there, the windows glowing with a false, warm, yellow light. High clouds, tinged moon-white, are sliding across the sky. I let the wind push me up the street like a scrap of trash. The moon watches, brushing everything around me with streams of silver from a quarter of a million miles away. None of this beauty is meant for me. I can see it, and I can feel it, but I can't feel it with another person. It's a cold beauty that's just there whether anyone is looking or not. I'm just one of the billion random things around the world lit up by that same cold light.

Lucky told me he goes out on the trail almost every night. I told him he shouldn't be ashamed of being tested for drugs. I told him his stepfather wasn't so bad – though he's still a complete geek compared to his real father. Lucky doesn't know why I shook and hung on to him in the car all the way back from the drug test. I'm not telling anybody about Johnson. I want to see Lucky right now. I want to feel Lucky's arms around me, right now, this time not out of pity but because he likes me or something. There's got to be some purpose for this gorgeous moon. I walk in its light to the trail.

Lucky, Rat and a few other boys are lounging around a tiny fire, the flames lighting up their faces from below and glinting off the dark whiskey bottle they pass around. Everything beyond the circle is dark. Rat is smoking a joint, sighing like he's so happy. The crackling of the burning twigs is the only sound in the woods. I find them here by instinct, feeling my way down the trail through the silvery brush. Then, after the trees crowd out even the moonlight overhead, I see the fire and hear them laughing. They make a little spot like they've been waiting for me. I put a few more twigs on the fire.

"Not too much, man. We're going skating soon."

I turn down a sip of whiskey. I'm not going to put my mouth on the top of the same bottle they've been using. They're talking and laughing with each other, but in the stupid way guys do, all insults and coolness.

"How'd you get out of the house?" It's Lucky.

"You don't know my house."

They all laugh like they know exactly what I mean. They act like I'm one of them, but the truth is I would be afraid if Lucky weren't here. Rat is holding his own tattooed arms, shivering. I'm the only person who notices he's wearing just a T-shirt with the sleeves cut off.

"Wanna hit?" Rat passes his joint to Lucky, who just holds it in his fingers and stares. I take it out of his hands and drag on it. I know you have to get it down your lungs, but it explodes in my chest into a horrible cough. They laugh at first, but my coughing goes on for too long. Finally I stop. My eyes are full of tears and the back of my throat is raw.

"This is worse than the dry heaves." The words are strained out of my throat.

Rat snickers, and the sound of his laugh holds itself in my head for a long time, and it's fascinating, and I'm concentrating on that sound like there's a meaning in it. I feel like I've been staring at the fire for too long, and I turn to look at Lucky and

Oh

My

God

is he beautiful. I can only look at one thing at a time, but t okay. I look at Rat and he's smiling, his goose-bumped, mus arms beautiful in their own way. I look at the other guys, and whiskey bottle, and the fire. Each is just what it is, as if it's waiting my whole life for me to really see it. The joint drops f my hands and I look for it on the ground but can't find it, even that just makes me laugh. The guys laugh too, and I fir feel like I am getting the big joke that's underneath everyth the joke that nobody outside of this circle really understand

Rat jumps up and down holding his arms.

"I am so freaking cold!"

"Maybe you should have worn some clothes." I can't laughing. I think I'm so funny.

"Maybe you should take yours off and lend them to me

"That's not gonna happen." Funny again.

"I'm too cold. Gotta go."

Rat and another guy go off. We hear them crashing aro in the bushes for so long we're thinking they must be lost, then we hear their skateboards rumbling down the trail. I c over next to Lucky.

"How'd you get out, really?"

"My father's gone into a coma or something. He's just sta at the wall."

"My mother's out working until midnight. She has her trial tomorrow."

"What's it about?"

"Some company says they paid too much on some deal.

"Are they right?"

"She says it doesn't matter who's right if you're lawyer."

The fire has pretty much burned out and the moonligh coming in again through the woods around us. The embers hissing, swelling and shrinking like they're breathing themsel Lucky is still here. There must be some way to get his a it. Maybe the "almost" is the important part. Maybe Mr. Folsom is trying to say you should find something real between yourself and the blackness and then just go for it.

I look at Dad with his head down, working on his papers. The cold quiet coming off of him fills that room like an invisible poison gas, and it starts to creep up around my ankles and fill up this room too. It's really simple. I have to run for my life. Dad is so out of it I don't need to sneak out. I even open the hallway closet to pick up my coat.

Outside, the street is empty. The moon is etched with soft white mountains. The houses are just dark shapes closed against all those who don't belong in there, the windows glowing with a false, warm, yellow light. High clouds, tinged moon-white, are sliding across the sky. I let the wind push me up the street like a scrap of trash. The moon watches, brushing everything around me with streams of silver from a quarter of a million miles away. None of this beauty is meant for me. I can see it, and I can feel it, but I can't feel it with another person. It's a cold beauty that's just there whether anyone is looking or not. I'm just one of the billion random things around the world lit up by that same cold light.

Lucky told me he goes out on the trail almost every night. I told him he shouldn't be ashamed of being tested for drugs. I told him his stepfather wasn't so bad – though he's still a complete geek compared to his real father. Lucky doesn't know why I shook and hung on to him in the car all the way back from the drug test. I'm not telling anybody about Johnson. I want to see Lucky right now. I want to feel Lucky's arms around me, right now, this time not out of pity but because he likes me or something. There's got to be some purpose for this gorgeous moon. I walk in its light to the trail.

Lucky, Rat and a few other boys are lounging around a tiny fire, the flames lighting up their faces from below and glinting off the dark whiskey bottle they pass around. Everything beyond the circle is dark. Rat is smoking a joint, sighing like he's so happy. The crackling of the burning twigs is the only sound in the woods. I find them here by instinct, feeling my way down the trail through the silvery brush. Then, after the trees crowd out even the moonlight overhead, I see the fire and hear them laughing. They make a little spot like they've been waiting for me. I put a few more twigs on the fire.

"Not too much, man. We're going skating soon."

I turn down a sip of whiskey. I'm not going to put my mouth on the top of the same bottle they've been using. They're talking and laughing with each other, but in the stupid way guys do, all insults and coolness.

"How'd you get out of the house?" It's Lucky.

"You don't know my house."

They all laugh like they know exactly what I mean. They act like I'm one of them, but the truth is I would be afraid if Lucky weren't here. Rat is holding his own tattooed arms, shivering. I'm the only person who notices he's wearing just a T-shirt with the sleeves cut off.

"Wanna hit?" Rat passes his joint to Lucky, who just holds it in his fingers and stares. I take it out of his hands and drag on it. I know you have to get it down your lungs, but it explodes in my chest into a horrible cough. They laugh at first, but my coughing goes on for too long. Finally I stop. My eyes are full of tears and the back of my throat is raw.

"This is worse than the dry heaves." The words are strained out of my throat.

Rat snickers, and the sound of his laugh holds itself in my head for a long time, and it's fascinating, and I'm concentrating on that sound like there's a meaning in it. I feel like I've been staring at the fire for too long, and I turn to look at Lucky and

O h

M y

G o d

is he beautiful. I can only look at one thing at a time, but that's okay. I look at Rat and he's smiling, his goose-bumped, muscled arms beautiful in their own way. I look at the other guys, and the whiskey bottle, and the fire. Each is just what it is, as if it's been waiting my whole life for me to really see it. The joint drops from my hands and I look for it on the ground but can't find it, and even that just makes me laugh. The guys laugh too, and I finally feel like I am getting the big joke that's underneath everything, the joke that nobody outside of this circle really understands.

Rat jumps up and down holding his arms.

"I am so freaking cold!"

"Maybe you should have worn some clothes." I can't stop laughing. I think I'm so funny.

"Maybe you should take yours off and lend them to me."

"That's not gonna happen." Funny again.

"I'm too cold. Gotta go."

Rat and another guy go off. We hear them crashing around in the bushes for so long we're thinking they must be lost, but then we hear their skateboards rumbling down the trail. I crawl over next to Lucky.

"How'd you get out, really?"

"My father's gone into a coma or something. He's just staring at the wall."

"My mother's out working until midnight. She has her first trial tomorrow."

"What's it about?"

"Some company says they paid too much on some deal."

"Are they right?"

"She says it doesn't matter who's right if you're the lawyer."

The fire has pretty much burned out and the moonlight is coming in again through the woods around us. The embers are hissing, swelling and shrinking like they're breathing themselves. Lucky is still here. There must be some way to get his arms

53

around me.

"Teach me to skate."

Out on the trail, one of Lucky's friends has already crashed, dropping his flashlight – but then he pops up suddenly, cursing and laughing. Lucky does put his arm around my waist, but the whole deal is much more tippy than I expected and I'm grabbing onto him and my legs are lurching back and forth. Not the romantic scene I hoped for, but he really is showing me how to skate. He says if I step on and off the skateboard every time I get going too fast, I might make it to the bottom.

"Try it yourself now." He lets me go, but I hold tight to his hand, almost falling into him when the skateboard pulls away.

"Where?"

He points down the trail.

"You're kidding."

He isn't. I let go of his hand and wobble forward, my wheels rumbling. I can feel my skateboard's wheels moving on the hard surface, but it's so dark I can't really see anything below my knees. Right away I'm going too fast. If I put my foot on the ground now I'll do a split. I might as well try for a miracle. The cold air is rushing against my face. I'm going too fast to make the first turn, but I try it anyway, fantasizing about floating magically in and out of the moon shadows.

The skateboard stops dead and slams me into a bank, the earth punching me hard. My body's like in a straightjacket of pain and I can't take in any air. I know I'm dying, and it's so painful I just want it to be over. I can hear Lucky and the other guys run up. They can talk, so I know they can breathe, and I am so jealous of that. Lucky pulls me out of the bushes and helps me stand up, my mouth open and gasping for air that won't come.

"Kate, you'll be fine." Lucky doesn't know I can't breathe, and I can't tell him, because I can't talk. "You just got the wind knocked out of you. You'll be okay soon. Just hang on."

Just like Lucky says, my chest begins to let me take in little sips of air, but it will never be enough to live on. If I die, I want Lucky to be the last thing I see. In the time-stillness from the joint I smoked, my gasps at life are mixed up with visions of his face, like maybe I'm going to see this vision forever. For a long time it seems like I will die, but then somehow I can take in a little more air.

"I ... getting ..." It's so painful to talk. Why don't I just shut up?

"... better. It happens all the time. You just got the wind knocked out of you."

"No more ... skateboarding."

"I'll teach you in the daylight sometime." He's facing me, holding each of my hands hard like he thinks I'm going to fall over. The other guys have lost interest and are wandering away.

"No. Never."

"You'll be fine in five minutes, I promise you."

"Flashlights are too easy," Lucky is talking to the other guys, who are on their skateboards on the trail again. It might be five minutes or it might be an hour later and, just like Lucky said, I feel perfectly okay. I look at Lucky like Lazarus must have looked at Jesus when he raised him from the dead. Then he opens up his backpack and pulls out a whole collection of candles and hands one to each of us.

"We'll each carry one. And you got to keep it lit."

He sparks his lighter and lights my candle.

"Okay, but I'm not skating."

He just nods and takes the flame to the others, one by one.

So we go down slowly and together at first, the boys laughing and swearing each time a candle goes out, me walking behind. They stop where the trail drops down steeply and goes through a dark stand of tall trees so thick the moonlight is gone. I catch up to them, and we are all standing so close you can hear the flames sputtering in the breeze.

"Kate, take the flashlights out of my backpack and lay them ahead of us down there where the trail curves."

"What about my candle?"

He'll hold it for me. I hate to let it go, but I don't mind going ahead, figuring out the curve, planting the flashlight markers. Then I step back off the trail so I can see them all at once.

The line of hooded shapes glides towards me on the dark path. The shapes are all in a line, each skater hunched over his candle. At first I can't see the flames hidden behind their cupped hands. As the skaters get close to the curve, the candles seem to light up one by one. Then they all swing into the curve at the same time like a string of lanterns on a slow, rumbling, old-time train. It's eighty years ago and I am my grandmother from North Carolina watching the late train wind its way into the foothills. The train passes by, the candles are blocked from my view again, and everything melts into the sweet-smelling darkness.

When I catch up with them, they're looking down the last steep hill to the bridge. Rat has started a huge bonfire right on the trail down below, with black-edged flames and the smell of burning asphalt. Rat and another guy are off to the side, lying low on the ground to be away from the black smoke of their own fire. One of our guys tries to jump the flames but doesn't quite make it, and his skateboard flips a burning branch up and he goes into an amazing, sparking, twisting dismount in the woods. They laugh at me because I just walk all the way down and edge around the fire, jumping back whenever the greasy flames reach my way. Then, behind me, through the sizzling and bubbling sounds of the fire, I hear the sound of Lucky's skateboard. When he's almost into the fire, he just bumps his skateboard onto the dirt on the side of the trail and keeps going, bending his knees a little deeper.

Suddenly a log flies up in front of him. It hits him in the shins, and he tumbles and goes down so hard you can hear his body hit the dirt. He crumples down on the ground, grabbing his leg. Then Rat and his friend pop up, laughing.

"Ow! You bastards!" Lucky shouts.

"I saw that, you assholes!" One of the other guys runs at Rat, holding his skateboard like a club. Everybody else follows, but Rat stands his ground, smirking.

"You really hurt him," I shout.

"Christ, Kate. Take a joke. You took my weed. Don't act like I'm a criminal or something." Then he turns and disappears.

Lucky is saying he isn't hurt that bad, so we help him up the trail towards his mother's house. His leg gets gradually better, and soon he pulls away from us to show us that he can limp along by himself. It's sad that a little thing like a stick thrown in his path can drag him down so far from perfectly all right.

"How bad is it?"

"It's nothing. You can't have fun if you're afraid to get hurt."

Lucky's mother's house is across the stream and at the opposite end of the trail from the school. It's an old, brown, shingled house, pretty much surrounded by the woods, on top of a hill right near the trail. We all sit down in a row on a stone wall at the bottom of the hill, near the garage. At the front of the garage, near the high point, there's an old, green porch light shaped like a candy kiss. The bulb flashes on, and we hear Lucky's stepfather clip-clopping in his slippers down the long stone steps from the house in the dark.

"I was working on a project in the den and I didn't notice you were gone. Where have you been?"

"The trail." Lucky holds up his skateboard without looking at him.

"We had to practically carry him back! Rat threw a log at him! He almost fell in the fire!" One of the dumber guys.

"I just tripped. Tripped on a log. I'm okay now."

"Maybe you should come in, have me take a look at it in the light."

"No, I'm okay, really."

"I don't have any children of my own, Lucky." Stepfather Ralph launches into a speech. "But it seems to me that if you stayed home and did your homework, and worked on your problems, instead of going out and creating more, you might make things better for yourself." His voice drops off at the end because he knows no one's listening.

"Yeah ..." I can tell Lucky is going to say "whatever," but he changes his mind. "Yeah, thanks, Ralph."

Ralph sighs, looks up at the sky, and goes back up the stairs. Lucky goes quiet. When Lucky stops talking, everybody else stops too, and the other guys take off in different directions for home. After they leave, Lucky limps over and flicks the garage light off. He limps back toward me on his bad leg.

"Hey! I'm walking like Johnson now."

"Stop it!"

He looks at me real annoyed like I'm Ralph or something.

"Lucky, Johnson tried to rape me again today."

"What?"

"I got away. He's so stupid. But he still scares me up close."

He limps over.

"Jesus! Why didn't you tell me?"

"He came over to me in the hall while you were gone, and I thought maybe he was going to do some kind of retarded apology or something. He's so strong when he gets hot."

"You kicked his ass again? Yeah? That's great! That guy's a real sicko. Somebody's got to do something about him."

Behind Lucky, on the other side of the driveway, a shimmer of light slides through the shadows. I touch Lucky and point. We wait, holding our breath, and a doe finally steps out of the woods into the moonlight. She takes a few steps away on her graceful stick legs and puts her nose down toward the grass. Her coat glows silver.

"Oh." Lucky just breathes it.

I put my mouth up to his ear. "Thank you for showing me the woods. Ever since I was a kid, I knew it was so amazing here, but I forgot about it until tonight."

"It's so cool, and it's all around us, right next to us."

The doe lifts her head and listens. We are so still she doesn't see us, but suddenly she bolts like she's on springs. All we can see is her bright tail like a cool white flame bouncing its way up into the woods.

Lucky limps around in a circle in front of his garage, trying out his leg.

"That looks like a shaman's dance."

There's an actual rhythm to it.

"I'm calling the deer back, telling her we won't hurt her."

He stops in front of me.

"But that's a lie," he says. "We will hurt her."

"No, we won't."

"We're ripping down their woods every day to build more houses. Woods are nothing to some people but land, and land is nothing to them but a way to make money.

"Kate, do you ever think like I do sometimes, that the earth could stay so beautiful, with all the animals on it and all, if only there weren't any people?"

Right now I'm thinking two might be enough.

"I won't forget this night." I'm whispering like I think the stars are eavesdropping or something. Lucky doesn't say anything. He's squirming like he's uncomfortable.

"Will you tell me something, Kate?"

"Anything."

"Why did your parents split up?"

"I don't know. You said it happens to everybody."

"Yeah, but ... A split is one thing, but ..."

"... but what? What do you mean?"

"Kate, I have two houses. I have two parents who are fighting over me." He looks at me like I'm supposed to say something.

His voice goes lower, like he's worried about eavesdroppers too. "And, to tell you the truth, Ralph really isn't that bad a stepfather."

"But it still sucks, Lucky. I know it does."

"Yeah. It sucks. But what I mean is, it seems like your mother doesn't even want you. And that's got to be even worse."

Chapter 7

"Sam, I need to get this over with."

Clare and I were meeting at a neutral spot, a restaurant in Burkeville, the county seat, twenty miles away from Glenwood. The restaurant was just a mile from the County Recreation Department where I worked, but none of my coworkers ever ate there. The salads were sprinkled with gorgonzola cheese or pine nuts and invariably drizzled with raspberry vinaigrette, and everything came with carmelized onions. Nobody on the county payroll could afford that kind of stuff every day for lunch.

You had to pull off the street and into a high-rise parking garage to lunch here. I drove my van up the winding spiral to the top of the garage, then back down to the bottom, then back up. There were plenty of spaces, but I was looking for Clare's car, to get an idea in advance of where I would run into her. On the way down in the elevator, every lit button on the panel brought a Pavlovian mixture of fear and longing, and I held my breath every time the doors opened.

To my surprise, she was already seated at a table, waiting for me. We said hello gently enough, and she waited just a moment for me to get settled.

"To get this over with, Sam, I'm making you a genuine, specific offer. You can have the house – forever. You can have all of our four thousand in savings. You can have all of your pension. All I want is Alexander's Woods."

"What about Kate? Did you forget this one thing?"

When she was in her businesslike mode, Clare was not capable of being flustered. "I did not forget Kate, Sam. I know she prefers to be with you right now. I won't interfere, as long as I get some visitation."

"She says she doesn't want to see you."

"She will sooner or later, Sam. She'll remember who taught her to use the computer, who took her to the ballet, who took her to New York every year."

"Basically, you're saying you get Alexander's Woods or we fight it out with lawyers."

"Sam, I was thinking about what you said last time. About riding past Alexander's Woods every day, and how it haunts you with memories. But then I realized something: you have to go out of your way to ride past Alexander's Woods."

"I know. But if you lived there with Anton, I would ride past it every day anyway. I would have to."

Clare had been smoothing the white tablecloth with her steady fingers. She raised her businesslike green eyes and really looked at me for the first time. These were the intelligent eyes of the woman I lived with for sixteen years, and who really knew my soul. What those eyes showed then was boredom, coated with a thin layer of pity. Seeing myself reflected like that in the eyes of the only woman I'd ever loved, I had to hold on to the table to keep from floating away.

To stay sane, I knew, I should make a quick deal with her, then turn around, walk away and never look back. But every time I forced myself to blank out Clare from my soul, everything went black, and I couldn't even talk, not even to Kate. If I couldn't talk to Kate, I would lose her too. My only choice was to fight with Clare, if only to get from that fight the energy to go on.

Clare cleared her throat, took a drink of water and paused until she got my attention. "Sam, if it makes you feel any better,

I have no intention of building a house there or living there with Anton. I shouldn't tell you this, but it's a business deal. Anton has options on property around there. If we ... if he can get your tract, he can put together a large project, the last big development project in Glenwood."

"My mother looked into something like that years ago. The tract's too hilly, not big enough to make a go of it financially, and the zoning isn't right."

"Anton has connections with people in the county," she instructed me. As if I didn't know that Anton had been throwing his family's money around and sucking up to the local politicians for years, pretending he was a real businessman like his father.

"He thinks he can do this, Sam, and I want to help him."

"Clare, if this scheme goes through ... I hope you're going to get your share, in your own name."

"Don't insult me, Sam," she bristled.

"Good. You'll take care of yourself. You'll get your cut. Don't roll your eyes, Clare. I didn't mean that in a bad way. You're a good businesswoman. I've always admired you for that."

Clare's eyes suddenly pleaded with me. My gaze was riveted to her face. What was it she wanted to confess?

"It's not all just business, Sam. Anton needs this project to go through, and I don't mean he needs this just financially. People don't know Anton like I do. They remember him from when he was just a young punk with too much money. People don't know how hard it is to always be compared to your father and to always come up short. He's grown, and he's worked hard for years, without much success. He tries hard. People don't realize that. And he needs this project, Sam. He needs it now. And I'm going to make it happen for him if I possibly can."

She was almost breathless by the end of her speech. A glow had come over her face, and her whole body was animated. The look in her eyes was sincere and concerned. I no longer had to guess what happened to the love light I used to see in them.

I didn't want more pity, so I steeled myself and continued to talk, and negotiate, as if this stuff happened every day. I guess it does. Maintaining my façade might have made me seem more rigid, but it was really all I could manage just then. She sighed and looked away from me and across the room.

"How did you get here?" I said idiotically. "I didn't see your car in the garage."

"Somebody drove me," she said, looking, it seemed, at a specific spot across the restaurant.

Suddenly I put one and one together. I followed her eyes and saw Anton standing at the bar.

"Oh Christ, Clare! You bring him even here, when we're talking about how to divide up our family?"

"You weren't supposed to see him. Oh, here he comes!" She stood up halfway, but Anton reached the table and grabbed a chair and pulled it around backwards and sat down on it before she could stop him.

"Sam," he said, and he didn't even have the sense not to use his hearty let's-make-a-deal tone. "I can see things aren't going too well."

"They haven't been going well for years," I said. "Now I know why."

"Stop this!" Clare whispered harshly, both of her hands on the table.

Anton leaned both of his elbows over the back of the chair and onto the table. "I think I can make this a little easier for the both of you." He looked strong and tanned, but there was a sour look on his lips that explained why he had never been the dealmaker his father was. "Whatever you're thinking about the woods, just add this to the deal. I will pay $100,000 an acre for that property. That's a good deal; half of it's so hilly it's good for nothing. I'll pay it to you directly. As long as I get it, I don't care. So you don't have to give it up as part of your divorce,

Sam. You can just sell it to me now for a good price."

"You're never getting it, asshole."

"I got connections in this county like you'll never have. All the way up. And you haven't even had to fight with the lawyers yet. Clare's been going easy on you, but she's got a really good set of lawyers."

"Yeah, and I bet you're paying for them."

"No. You're the one who will be paying for them, in the end."

"Why are you here?" I was shouting.

"Stop it, Sam. Sit down," Clare snapped.

"You're going to have to give it up." Anton was talking faster. "You can't split up with your wife and just keep everything."

"This is none of your fucking business! Just because you fuck my wife doesn't mean you can stick your nose into the rest of my business." Then I dumped the table on him.

Anton backed up so fast he bumped into the table behind him, and the whole restaurant went still. I could see the color rising in his face, deepening his tan. He wanted to come at me then, and I was hoping he would.

"Sam!" Clare yelled.

"You didn't have the balls to keep her." His voice was an animal grunt.

I took a step toward him. The manager appeared at Anton's side. I hardly heard what the manger said. Out of the corner of my eye I saw Clare get up and walk away. Anton stepped back, and his eyes shifted. As soon as I sensed he was looking for a way out, my rage crested and drained away.

"Okay," I said to the manger. "I'm sorry. I'll pay for this." My hands were trembling as I reached for my wallet.

"That's okay, sir. I just need you both to leave right now."

"I wasn't even dining here," Anton challenged him. "I'll go back to the bar."

"Sir? No ..."

But Anton did just that – went back to the bar and sat down. The manger shrugged. "Please get out," he said to me.

On my way out I saw Clare sitting alone, waiting for me on a metal chair in the waiting area of the restaurant. I had an instant testosterone-induced fantasy that she would see me in a new light now and choose me over Anton after all. She stood up and walked over to me. Do not believe or even hope that anything good is going to happen, I told myself.

"That won't happen again," she said.

"Don't bring him around any more."

"No. You don't understand, Sam. I will bring him around. If you want to talk to me about Kate or anything else, ever, you will not act like that. You will act civilly."

There was some truth in what she said. I would have to be trained to accept the thought of dealing with her and Anton forever. There would be severe punishment otherwise. But accepting it would not be enough humiliation. In the long run, I would not only have to accept it. I would also have to be trained to accept it gracefully.

I spiraled down the parking lot. At least Clare's car wasn't there. But then Anton's decorated Corvette swerved in front of me to line up first at the ticket booth, forcing me to slam on my brakes. There was nothing personal in this; it was just the way Anton drove. The top was down and she was sitting up smartly, smiling at him. If she noticed me she didn't show it.

Chapter 8

The girls are sitting in little groups, thinking up ways to be superior, and the boys are standing on the grass slapping each other or throwing stones into the trees. Ms. Nesbitt is sitting high up in the stands like a spectator at her own open-air English class. Finally it dawns on her that the kids are making too much noise to hear what she's trying to say. What did she expect? Did she think we were all going to like, get together on our own and ask for her guidance or something? Her face falls when it hits her that nobody's listening. All of a sudden she stands and stomps down the aluminum benches in her chunky shoes, her face closed off like she is in pain. She faces away from the stands and takes a couple gulps of air before she turns around towards the kids.

"Somebody say something." She's almost begging, and it's still hard to hear what she's saying at first. "I mean it. Something real, not something you think I want to hear. But something real."

Nobody says anything. How do you even know what's real?

"That's too hard, isn't it?"

Everybody is listening to her now, and she's not so upset. You can tell because that far-off look comes back into her eyes again.

"Let's go a little lighter. This is supposed to be fun. Let me hear a story, a new story. Come on, somebody be brave enough.

Begin with just a voice, a real voice, anything, a voice in your head. I mean it. Anything. Come on."

"I am the voice of mathematics," Johnny Gott holds his nose to impersonate Mr. Folsom's high-pitched voice. "I will teach you algebra, and that will somehow give you control over the moon. I can't go to the moon myself because my pansy hairdo will not fit in any of those space helmets."

"Shut up!" It's me, yelling out before I know what I'm doing. I don't know why Johnny can't hear Mr. Folsom's voice like I do, the patience in that voice and the little quaver that comes into that voice when Johnny blurts out the stupidest answers over and over and Mr. Folsom is trying so hard to be nice until it looks like he's going to crack. I'm screaming now and I can't stop myself.

"That's so stupid! He's so smart and you don't even understand what he's talking about. You don't even ... You ..."

The world goes dead quiet and everybody is looking at me. I can't say what I mean. I am such a dork. I put my head down and start walking away. Ms. Nesbitt says something, but she can't force me to stay. I'm trying to walk away but I'm not getting anywhere. I don't know what's happening to me, but it doesn't seem to be happening to anyone else and I don't understand why everything's changed and I don't fit in any more.

"See? Two real voices. You heard them, didn't you? You listened, didn't you? That's because we heard honest voices. Those voices are in all of us."

Diane catches up to me and puts her arm around my waist and turns me around. No one is looking at me. They're all looking at Ms. Nesbitt, all real quiet like they're thinking.

"Who's next?" she is saying.

"I want to hear those two argue," somebody says.

"Kate?" Ms. Nesbitt stares at me. So does everybody else. "Do you want to finish?"

Diane looks in my eyes and understands.

"I have a voice," Diane calls back. "I am the voice of the little brown rabbit hopping through the woods."

Everybody groans.

"Go ahead, smartasses, say something."

"Okay, I am the voice of the vicious hunter with a loaded shotgun shooting all the brown rabbits in the woods."

"You shoot just the brown ones?" Another voice.

"Why? Do you think I'm a racist hunter?"

"You nitwit," another kid says, "All rabbits in the woods are brown."

"No, they're not. I've seen grey ones."

"I've seen white ones."

"Not in the woods. You are so ignorant. Those white ones aren't real."

"Aren't *real*? Are you crazy?"

"I am the voice of the stream." Ms. Nesbitt's piercing voice shuts everybody up, and when we look at her, her red curls are shooting out like her head exploded. "I circle and sparkle and give life to everything in the woods. And the woods nurtured our souls even before our mothers were born."

People are really looking at her.

"Can't you feel it? The life rushing up through every blade of grass? 'The force that through the green fuse drives the flower.' It's the real thing that's in us all, and it's a million times better than TV or downloads. Find your voice, find your real voice.

"Don't be so scared. Pick a voice, any voice. Try one out. You might have to try a thousand voices before you find your own."

Lucky slowly stands up, his voice deep and soft and scary. "I am the voice of Johnson. My mind is twisted and I hate everybody who is normal."

"Lucky, cut it out. That's not funny."

"Who says our voices have to be funny? Can't anybody see? Johnson isn't going to stop."

69

But Lucky's voice does stop the whole class. Ms. Nesbitt stares at him like she's really thinking hard.

"It doesn't have to be funny," she says at last. "It doesn't have to be acceptable. We've heard some real voices today. Each of us should try to find our own."

Diane keeps her arm around my waist all the way back into the school, ignoring the stupid dork murmuring "lesbo" at us from behind. Inside, the air is stuffy with the smell of too many bodies too close together, and she pulls away. I know that I love her, not in the lesbo way but I know I'd follow her anywhere, she's just so cool.

"Kate, bring Lucky over to my house tonight. My parents are out of town. We need to party."

"I'm not really going with him or anything, Diane."

"For God's sake, Kate. He's hot, and I know you're into him."

"Really, I don't even know if he likes me."

"I don't want it to be just Carl and me all the time. Please? If Lucky won't come, find somebody else."

Mr. Folsom's shaggy head floats above the mad rush of kids changing classes, and then I recognize that voice calling out my name. It's a thin little voice, but the funny thing is I can always hear it now, even with a million people rushing around.

"Kate, you failed the last quiz on simultaneous equations."

"No!"

"They're not that hard, for someone as talented as you. I thought for a while this morning that you were really focusing again."

I can hear he's disappointed. It's not like I really care that much about math, but he cares. I'm the only one who knows he's not a complete loser, and he's the only one who thinks that I'm not a complete loser, and so we have this one thing in common, and if he thinks I'm good at math I might as well play along.

"You're good at this, Kate, but you need to understand simultaneous equations. Come to my classroom after school. You can learn it in 20 minutes."

The next class, Wellness, is an easy one. There's never any homework. Last time a couple of kids demonstrated swing dance moves the whole period. Ms. Davis always sits in the back of the room with the last bank of lights turned out. Today we're having a demonstration of a little transparent plastic doll, Smokin' Suzie, who has a little motor that smokes a cigarette until her lungs get all brown inside. This is the third time we've seen it, and there's still a little smoke halo around her head from the class just before us. Lucky comes in and says hi to some guys, but he sits down next to me.

"Ms. Nesbitt is being fired."

"For being crazy?"

"For the outdoor classes."

It hits me that this gorgeous boy is talking to me like a normal person.

"I don't think they can do that," I say. He shrugs and looks away. "Why do you think it's funny that Johnson's attacking me?"

"I think it's horrible, what he did to you. Somebody should kick his ass good. But everybody's acting like it didn't happen. It's not funny. I'm sorry."

"How is your leg?"

"It'll be fine. Hey, know what I did to Ralph last night? He made me show him the bruise. It was really ugly. He started saying like, if my mother was there would she take me to the emergency room? And I'm all 'Gee, I don't know. It kind of hurts a lot.' And every time he tries to tell himself it's just a bruise I say 'Gosh, Ralph, it does really hurt a lot. Do you think maybe it's broken? Does it look like it's swelling up to you?' And he knows its not but he's so scared of my Mom he starts pacing back and forth, pushing his glasses up on his face. Then, honest to God, he starts sweating."

"You're so evil."

"Yeah, but then he starts talking about calling the police on Rat, and then I'm the one who's sweating."

"Did he do that, call the police?"

"I had to stop that."

"How?"

"It wasn't easy. I had to tell him a huge lie. I said Rat was my best friend."

Just when I'm getting ready to ask him to go with me to Diane's party, something goes wrong with Smokin' Suzy, and Ms. Davis tells us the class is over. I hunt Lucky down in the hall, and I get to him before he starts talking with his friends, but at the last minute I chicken out about the party.

"After school, will you teach me to skate?"

"I have detention after school. The cops are coming to ask me Rat's real name."

"Why?"

"Somebody else called the cops. I think it was Greg's father."

"But why you?"

"I'm the guy the cops know, Kate. They always want me to tell them about somebody else. Rat thinks I tell them everything. That's why he hates me."

"I have detention too, math detention."

"I'll come get you."

Two other kids are in the after-school class with Mr. Folsom. He is right about how easy simultaneous equations are. At least the ones with only three variables.

"Fine, you pass this. I can't see how you got them wrong in the first place."

"I wasn't thinking about math then."

"Are you having problems?" He stands right at my desk.

"Just a lot of stuff."

"Teaching is a lot of stuff sometimes. Did you hear that discussion of multiplicative inverses today?"

"Johnny Gott's not really stupid like he acts. He just doesn't get it that you're supposed to actually think."

"So you defend that guy who tries to gross out every girl in the class?"

"I ..."

"I'm not criticizing you for that. I think you're a really fine person to be so loyal to your classmates. So, Kate, what have you been worrying about?"

"My parents are ... probably splitting up."

"Oh, that's hard, Kate, that's really hard. Believe me, I know first-hand how hard that is."

"Did it happen to you?"

"In a way."

I don't ask him what that means. I don't want to be talking about this. Actually, this is the first time I've ever said the words, splitting up, even to myself. It feels like I just stepped off a cliff or something.

"Can I go now? I have to meet a friend."

"We have to do four variables now. Oh. Okay, I guess we can do it some other time. Go be with your friend."

Lucky's in the hallway, but he shrugs his shoulders to everything I say until we're out the door.

"The cops didn't show. Let's go down the trail before they change their mind. You won't believe what's going on. I heard Freeland on the phone. He promised some senator the whole school will be torn down by March 31st."

"What! Why?"

"I don't know. I was talking to Ms. Cascio. She was telling me all about her daughter, and I didn't get to pick up Freeland's line until the very end."

Lucky always hides his skateboard a little way off the trail. Today, there are two. One of them is aquamarine, faded and scratched.

"Why do you have two?"

"In case you would come."

So now I'm falling off some other kind of cliff. It's funny, you go along and it's nothing after nothing day after day, and then suddenly it's not.

"I'm sorry you got hurt last night."

"Last night was tight. I liked every part of last night, Kate."

He got the aquamarine one from his cousin last summer and put new wheels on it last night, after he got home with an injured leg, after he finished messing with Ralph. He was thinking of me after he got home with his injured leg, after he finished messing with Ralph.

"I can show you better today, in the light."

"How hard can it be if Rat can do it?"

"Actually, Rat can't do it very good. That's why he always starts something else – like fires."

A new layer of crunchy green leaves has blown across the trail and is lying over the honeysuckle all around. The tiny trees on either side have curling, teardrop leaves wiggling in the wind.

I'm a complete klutz at first, but it's only a matter of balance, something I'm pretty good at. Then I get too smart and try to do one of Lucky's fancy turns and end up flat on my butt in the honeysuckle at the side of the trail. Lucky is behind me, and I hear a lot of wheel grinding and leaf crunching as he flies by me, does a 180, stops dead and kick-flips his board up into his hands.

"That's great!" he says. "You've basically got it!" He's smiling at me like I just qualified for the Olympics.

I laugh so hard I lie back in the leaves and just hope I can stop before I wet my pants. He makes it worse by coming over and looking down at me so seriously. The sunlight is blinding, and he is just a giant silhouette of a face above me, with deep black eyes. Then he kneels down next to me and the sun lights up his skin and he is as beautiful as a painting, a precious kind of painting you would not dare to touch.

"Kate, come to my father's house with me later."

"Why?" Why doesn't really matter. I'm coming.

But why later?

He doesn't answer. We wander down toward the stream for a while without talking. The wind shimmers all the colors around us, and the tall trees creak overhead. Soon, down close to the bridge, we step into the rough patch of asphalt made by Rat's bonfire the night before. Lucky finds the log that Rat threw in his path last night, but then he goes right past it, crouches down and stares at the ground.

"What?"

"See that stuff Rat was lying in last night? Poison ivy."

A deep cracking boom, like a lightning strike right up the hill, makes us both jump.

"What's ...?"

"A gun. A rifle."

It happens again, and it seems closer. Lucky grabs my arm and drags me down the bank of the stream and pushes me under the bridge.

"Squinch higher up, under the wood, so he won't see us."

"Who is it?"

"I'm almost sure it's Rat."

"Do you think he'd shoot us?"

"Not on purpose. But maybe he's drunk, or crazy with poison ivy."

Just when I think he must have gone away, I hear a much closer rifle crack. Then there are a lot of footsteps on the bridge, then Rat's voice.

"Throw it."

Somebody throws a bottle down in the grass at the edge of the stream just below where we are. For a second I can see the sunlight on the glass, then there is another crack that shakes the bridge. A glop of water and mud shoots back up from the stream and hits me in the face. I don't know if I've been shot or what's going on, but Lucky holds me to him and whispers that I'm okay. It's only mud.

"Shit! Damn!" The mud must have hit Rat too. He's mad, but the boys with him are laughing. They go up the trail that Lucky and I have just come down, and a minute later we hear another crack coming from farther away.

Lucky wipes the mud off my face with his shirt. You can still smell the sharp smell of rifle smoke under the bridge. I am not embarrassed that he's cleaning my face, that we're standing ankle-deep in mud, or that he held me a minute ago. It all seems as natural as the stream, which has already recovered and is now flowing crystal clear, or the rocks slippery with moss, or the bottle that Rat didn't even hit still glinting in the sun.

"Let's go to your father's place right now."

He says no, but then there's another crack and he says let's go. He doesn't stop at the top of the hill overlooking his father's back yard. He goes right down to the fence. The two dogs come out and make a huge fuss. One of them, the big purplish retriever, throws himself in the air over and over, no matter how many times Lucky pushes him down. The black lab just walks over and noses into us.

"Is he old? He's so fat."

"Duke? She's pregnant."

"*Duke* is pregnant?"

"I named her when she was a puppy. Guess I didn't check her out too good."

The purple dog, Molson, finally stops jumping, except every once in a while he leaps up and tries to lick my face. He loves it when I ruffle the fur behind his ears. Whenever I talked about getting a puppy, Mom and Dad always said I deserved one but we didn't have the kind of place a dog would need to be happy. Lucky's father's place is exactly the kind of place a dog would need to be happy.

We have to get through the dogs and weave around the birdhouses and wagon wheels and other decorations in the back yard. Each wooden step up to the deck has potted plants on it. There's like an open roof over the deck with plant pots and wooden birds and metal stars and suns hanging down. Up close, the stars are dull, like they've been out in the weather too long. They aren't the tiny points of light like the stars in my imagination, but they are right in front of your face here, and you can touch them.

I don't know what I expected Earl's girlfriend to look like – but she's practically Lucky's stepmother, so I guess she wasn't supposed to be so hot. She opens the door in bare feet and tight jeans and walks back across the kitchen like a model while she shakes out her thick auburn hair.

"You guys been playing in the mud? Come here, hon, let me help you get that smudge off your face." She dabs at me with a sponge from the kitchen sink, holds me at a distance like she's a great makeup artist. "There. I won't ask you all how that happened."

"Kate's a friend. This is Rudi."

"Let me at you now."

Lucky brushes her hands off and turns away.

"Was that you shooting that rifle in the woods today?"

"No! Not us. Rat. We had to get out of the woods because of that."

"Your Daddy's not here. He's putting brakes on his truck. One of his friends took him to get pads. He's got to take me to work, and I got to get ready to go."

"We'll just wait out on the porch."

"No you won't. Kate, don't listen to that gloomy-face guy. Come on in and set yourself in the living room while I get ready to go."

Watch her get ready to go is what it seems. She brushes out

77

her hair – it takes a lot of room to do this – then she uses a dark TV screen as a mirror and puts it up in a thick French braid. She's all graceful and quick.

"We had a little argument. He was hot when he left. I got to be at work in a half hour. You all want something to drink?"

The room is as wide as the house, with a window on each side. A little breeze wanders through. Hundreds of knick-knacks crowd every flat surface. Do I smell pot in the air? Then I hear a crunching sound coming from outside, then the sound of little bits of gravel hitting the side of the house. A truck slides to a stop in the driveway, and Lucky jumps to the window.

"Got the pads?"

"Yeah. Hey, boy. Let me get these things on real quick before it gets dark. Then you and I can take Rudi to work."

"I got Kate with me."

"Alright! Bring her too!"

Rudi's still working on her hair. She's has the sexy kind of look that makes every guy do a double-take. Lucky is still looking the other way, out the window.

"The reason your Daddy and I are fighting is over you."

Earl's eyes appear just above the sill of the window, straining to see through the screen.

"Yeah, we're fighting. But I can't stay mad at that woman for long. Lord knows I tried."

Chapter 9

Nesbitt was young, thin, fast moving, her arms all angles, her hair a mop of wild red curls. Her bold print dress was too big to look sexy.

"How could Kate be drinking until she's sick, and nobody at this school even knew about it?"

"The kids knew, Mr. Alexander. I asked a couple of them today. They all knew." I couldn't tell if Ms. Nesbitt was looking at me or Mr. Folsom, the math teacher, who had a chair next to mine. Folsom was a tall, skinny guy with long bony fingers that seemed to be always in motion. "At least Kate told other kids about it. The kids who keep their problems from everybody are the ones I worry most about."

"Why didn't the teachers notify me that she missed so many classes?"

"We did." Folsom's voice was thin too, his eyes exhausted. "I sent you an e-mail, and a letter home. I guess you never got them."

Did Clare get them and not tell me? All the past few weeks, while I was trying so hard not to crack, forcing myself ahead, did I close myself down so much that I missed all these messages? I hung my head, focused on my shoes, trying not to explain to these two young teachers the whole sad story of Clare and Kate and me.

"It's Kate's problem," I said, "it's our family's problem. It's not the school's problem if she cuts class."

"There's nobody else home during the day, right?" Nesbitt piped in. "There's an easy explanation. The kids get the letters first and tear them up. They erase the phone messages, even the e-mails. It happens all the time."

Folsom looked surprised too. "Anyway, Mr. Alexander, she's a good kid. She's making up her math work. She'll do fine."

"Thank you. I can call you directly to see how she's doing, right?" They both nodded, and I felt better. At the same time it seemed like I was getting away with something, ending this conference without confessing the terrible split in our family that probably was behind all of Kate's crazy behavior.

"I guess I need to talk to the principal too."

"Oh." They looked at each other. "Yes, you could do that."

"What?"

"Nothing," Nesbitt stammered. "We just don't know him very well." She stared in the direction of Folsom, I think.

"He's new," Folsom added. He wouldn't look at Nesbitt, who then shook her curls and talked out of the side of her mouth to me.

"He was sent here suddenly by the administration. The rumor is he was sent here just to do a favor for somebody higher up. I shouldn't be saying this."

"All we really know is, we can't get his attention when we talk about the kids."

"I want to talk to him anyway."

Principal Freeland had to talk to me because I was the parent of a kid who had been attacked. He sat back in his big chair and looked across the desk toward me, comfortable, maybe even cocky. I'm sure parents generally don't come back, a few days after a big conference, unless something has gone wrong again.

"I just found out Kate was drinking in the woods, and she missed most of her classes for almost two weeks, and nobody from the school told me."

"Oh."

"I should have known myself. I should have paid more attention. I'm not blaming the school for that."

"We can't control what happens in those woods."

"Johnson attacked Kate again yesterday, in the school."

"My God! Why didn't she report it?"

"She said there was no point."

Freeland edged back a little.

"There weren't any witnesses?"

"No."

"This could be a tough one."

"Not for me."

Freeland sized me up. I had threatened to call the police before, but I hadn't done it. He knew I didn't want to call in outside people, make things messier and more public. He knew I wanted the school to be an extension of the family, wanted to keep all of these problems within that family. He knew I was weak.

"There's not much we can do."

"Why not? Put special security on this Johnson guy? Or at least a tutor for Kate so she never has to see that cretin again."

"We can't treat that boy like he's a criminal. You saw it. He's got lawyers threatening lawsuits every time we move his desk."

"How about some help for Kate?"

"We just don't have the resources. That's the code word for money, Mr. Alexander."

"You don't have to tell me. I work for the government too."

"Then you understand. We had to beg the PTA to buy us a working water fountain. Now we're begging them for money for a copying machine. We can't afford one extra pencil for the average student in this school. There's no way we could pay for tutoring for Kate."

Nothing was going to be done about this Johnson kid. Nothing was going to be done to help Kate. I told myself it was better to have found out the truth, even if the truth was a stone wall. How did Freeland know I was so weak? How did Clare know? Maybe the bigger question was how had I convinced myself for fifteen years that I was a man.

"In that case, I have to ask you not to mention what I've said either."

"Said about what?"

"About Kate being attacked again. Or about her drinking in the woods."

"You want me to keep it quiet? Quiet from whom?"

"From Clare, my wife."

He cocked his head and looked down at me, and a little smile stole across his face. Could he see into the vault of depression and weakness that was at the core of me?

"And the reason for this request is ...?"

"As a personal favor. Could you just do this one thing for me, leave Clare out of this?"

The little smile came back.

"I should tell you the whole story. Kate's mother doesn't know half the problems Kate's been having. And there's a reason she shouldn't know."

Freeland said nothing, but his eyes were fixed on me. Those judgmental eyes made me want to confess even more. I wanted so much for there to be a higher power, a benevolent father to tell me it was all right. Maybe I wanted it so badly that I created one out of the bullying bureaucrat looking down at me from behind his massive desk. But even as I was telling him my sad story, even as I was giving up and letting this wave of sorrow roll over me and crash into the room and wash over both of us, I recognized the coldness in those eyes, and I was afraid I was lost now more than ever.

Chapter 10 ⬿

By the time Lucky's father gets the truck fixed, the sun has gone down and the sky has spread all out above us like a rippled fuchsia sheet. Lucky wants me to ride in the back with him in the bed. Better than squeezing in with Rudi. Lucky's father drags out a huge piece of cloth splattered with paint, folds it over a few times and spreads it out carefully in the bottom of the bed like he's expecting a hillbilly queen or something.

"It ain't exactly legal, Kate, so you might have to duck down once in a while."

I hang onto the metal sides and we squeak and bounce our way out of the driveway and out of this forgotten valley under the high power lines. Nobody lives here but Earl and Rudi and the people who live in a few other houses that look like they might have been put up by mistake. This is one of the weirdest things I've ever done, but Lucky sits back across from me and warms me with those eyes and it seems like this is just where I should be right now.

"We're going to the school first."

"Why?"

"I want Dad to tell me if it's really going to be torn down."

Soon we're there, but seeing the school kind of breaks the spell for me. I dread going back there tomorrow. There's now a big machine on the grounds, but down near the street. Lucky's father doesn't even slow down.

"Yeah," he yells back through the sliding window. "That's a post-hole digger. They'll be putting up a fence. You don't put up a fence in front that way except you're going to tear something down."

"They're tearing down the soccer stands." The truck's already moving faster and I'm not sure Earl can hear me. "Right? I mean Lucky told me they're paying you to do that."

"This's got nothing to do with the soccer stands. Looks to me like the whole school's going to be torn down."

"What for? What for?" He hears me because he slides the window open again.

"I'll ask around. Right now, Rudi and I got to finish our argument."

He drives out into Broward County and past a lot of nicer developments with really big, new houses jumbled next to each other on flat land. He keeps going for miles until there are actually farmers' fields with corn and stuff. There's a jet trail across the dying purple sky. One star appears just above the tops of the cornstalks.

"Duck!"

"What?"

"Duck! Cops! I mean it!"

Lying down with Lucky in the back of that ridiculous, squeaky truck, I can't stop laughing. The meaner the look Lucky tries to give me, the harder I laugh. The truck stops at a light and the police car pulls up next to us.

"I really don't want them to see this." Lucky pulls a baggie of pot from his pocket. "Rudi gave it to me on the way out."

"Put it away!" Dad would be so pissed if I got picked up for riding in a truck way out here. But mostly I'm thinking about Lucky and how much real trouble he could get in now for having pot. It doesn't seem funny any more.

The stoplight seems to last forever. I'm dreading seeing flashing blue lights. But nothing happens. The cops are probably ogling Rudi's thick French braid. Earl edges forward and stops, edges forward and stops, making the engine vibrate like he's going to race them. I can hear the police car move up even with us each time.

"We're okay," Lucky whispers.

There's a horrible screeching tire sound, but we're still there, not moving.

"I knew it. They had to beat us off the light."

Earl goes slowly through the intersection, and a few minutes later the truck stops outside a one-story brown wooden bar on a dusty parking lot on the edge of a cornfield. The sky has lost all its colors but deep blue, and a few more stars are out. Earl comes around, and I can't believe he wants us to go in.

"We'll stick you underage kids in a corner where nobody will notice."

Earl opens the side door wide and the four of us rush in with a blast of cold outside air. The men at the bar facing us, like cold-blooded reptiles staring out at us from across a prehistoric marsh, don't even blink. Earl puts us in a booth where I have to stretch my neck just to see the bar, but I do, especially when Rudi steps up behind it. Earl sits at the bar with a glass of water. There are a few tables, a couple of other booths and a pool table under a cloud of smoke. Two men in dirty jeans are leaning over the pool table and studying it like they're reading the future. There are a few men and even a couple of women at the tables.

"Why does Rudi take all that trouble fixing herself up to work in this dump? She could weigh 300 pounds in here and it wouldn't make any difference."

"I guess men always like to look at a hot woman."

I wouldn't know. I make myself think of that skateboard that Lucky fixed up for me, late last night. Rudi, I have to admit, looks smart and cool standing behind the bar, talking to Earl and tapping the top of the bar with her fingernails. She keeps her eye on the crowd, and when someone wants a drink she glides over and stoops down and takes their order and is gone before they can give her any trouble. With her stunning hair and long, tight jeans and bare midriff, she doesn't even look like she's the same species as me.

"Everything in this booth is sticky."

I look at him. "Let's go outside."

You can already see the wide yellow moon at the edge the sky. First we try to sit in the cab, but it's really dark and there's clanky metal stuff piled on the floor almost to the level of the seat.

"Let's get out and sit in the back."

Out in the moonlight, Lucky's face seems more molded, maybe hollower and not so magically handsome as it looked on the trail this afternoon. I feel like I can say anything to him now.

"What's going to happen to you, Lucky?"

"Good things." His smile is wonderful.

"What will Rat do if you give his name to the police?"

"I would never do that."

"What will the police do to you then? What if they find the pot that Rudi gave you? Why is she still giving you pot, anyway?"

"It's cool, but I know it's bad. She's bad. My Dad really loves her, though."

"My mother told me she left us because she's in love with her boyfriend."

"There's so much bad stuff going around ... I don't know."

We're wrapped in the tarp lying next to each other. The sky is now a deep grey-blue, with beds of stars floating behind veils of thin clouds. His face is right up to mine, and I can see him look at me and smile like he's happy. I think he is, right now. I'm already shaking a little bit – I think from the cold – and I want to touch him so bad, but I'm afraid I'll go into some kind of seizure if I do.

"My Dad is telling Freeland today that Johnson groped me again."

"Why don't you just call the cops? The school's never going to put him out."

"I don't know. My Dad wants to talk to Freeland. But I know the school won't do anything."

"Somebody has to get rid of Johnson."

I'm not as scared of Johnson as I was before. It's because of all the things I did since then. I got away from him a second time. I skateboarded down the trail in the dark, then learned to do it right the next the day. I got away from Rat and his rifle. And I figured out that Rudi was weird before I ever set foot in that house. None of these things are ever taught to you in school. School is just for the easy things, things that somebody else already knows the answer to. What I really need to know are the things I have to learn by myself.

"You're cold." He tries to pull the tarp closer around me, but his leg touches mine and I jump up and in a second I'm standing in the parking lot, at the very edge, stopped by a line of dry corn stalks outlined like black skeletons against the sky. They're whispering and crackling in the breeze. There is nowhere to run. I'm at the very edge of the suburbs and there's nothing beyond here but plant life. I hear Lucky's footsteps crunching towards me.

"What?" I snap at him before he even gets close.

"What's wrong? Do you need to go home? I'll get my Dad."

He puts his hand on my back as we're walking toward the truck, and his touch starts a weakness that spreads down my back and legs so I can hardly wobble forward. I put my hands on the metal of that black truck whose hundreds of white scratches suddenly seem so familiar to me.

"I shouldn't have brought you out here. You're so far above ... I'm sorry you had to see my messed-up life."

"It's not that. I love your life. I love the way you and your Dad are fighting to keep together ..."

I turn around to him, but he takes half a step back and he is gorgeous, gorgeous in the light that comes from the higher, whiter moon.

"Kate, you don't know everything about me."

"I know enough." My soul is breathing prayers to bring him back across the little cold gap between us.

His soul must feel mine calling because he does come back. He puts his hand on my waist, but he holds himself a little ways off. I know I'm going to die if he doesn't either kiss me or push me away. I raise my face to him. My lips are almost begging.

Chapter 11

Earl drives us back with the headlights turned off because he wants to show us how bright the moon is. The three of us are jammed together with the engine throbbing underneath and the heater blowing and both windows open. Lucky is holding my hand. I love the way Earl and Lucky just naturally understand each other without talking that much. Earl talks to me a little, real nice, like I'm his oldest friend. But everybody gets real quiet when we leave the cornfields and the open sky behind and the houses clump together on both sides around us. I make them drop me off at the sidewalk in front of my house. I'm not the same person who walked out that door this morning.

The house is dark inside, but I know Dad is here because I saw his car in the driveway. Then I see something white flickering in the dining room and I jump like it's a ghost, but it's only Dad's white shirt. He's slumped over the dining room table, watching a little TV he's set up in there. He didn't hear me come in the door, and he doesn't say anything when I say hi. His elbows are still propped on the table and he's still watching the news in the dark.

I switch on the light.

"Oh, hi, Kate. Can you turn that off?"

"It's dark!"

"Turn it off, please."

I do.

He's still looking at the TV. It's not like he's a news freak or anything. I take his hand.

"Dad, something really nice happened to me today, with Lucky."

Maybe you're not supposed to tell your father, but I was wondering if he ever had this feeling with Mom – maybe a long time ago. I must be such a baby to think it's such a big thing.

"Oh no, you didn't. Tell me you didn't, Kate."

"No, I didn't have sex with him, Dad."

Now he looks at me.

"He taught me to skate."

He pulls me against him and hugs me so hard I can feel him sobbing. I'm crying too. My face is pressed against his shoulder and I'm crying onto on his shirt.

"Lucky's a good friend. From what I've seen, I like the guy."

He smells just like he used to, that slightly sweaty man smell under the starched shirt. To me, that is the smell of a man who loves you. I squeeze him; I need him so bad. If Lucky smelled like this I would dissolve into a puddle.

"Why were you sitting here in the dark?"

"Sometimes when I'm alone I don't want to see the things here, the wallpaper, the furniture, things that remind me ..."

"... of Mom. Dad, if she wants to come back, I'll try not to be so snotty to her."

"It wasn't you. You were always wonderful, Kate. It wasn't you."

I hold him tighter.

"She hates me."

"Don't say that! Don't ever say that. It's not true."

"I love you, Dad." I bury my face in his neck. Just hold me.

He doesn't say anything back. He lets go of me while I'm still trying to hold him tight. I'm still holding on, pressing against him, but he's letting me go. I lean on him but he puts his hands on my shoulders and pushes me away, definitely pushes me away. And then I'm standing there shaking like a baby and he turns away from me and he stares at the television and doesn't say anything.

I'm out in the dark kitchen lit only by the stove-top light, blowing my nose and drinking a glass of water.

I do know I'm not the only one she hurt.

"Dad, can I fix you a hamburger or something? Spaghetti?"

"No thanks."

"Can you help me with my algebra later tonight?"

"Maybe another night. Okay?"

Carl drives right past the house like I told him to. I slip out the side door and meet him at the corner.

"Nice. This is your own car?"

"Camaro. Four years old. Got it for fifteen grand."

"You have, like, a full-time job?"

"Yeah. Nights."

He describes every part of the car like I'm going to buy it or something. It turns out that not one feature is exactly his first choice for that particular thing. Carl has a round face and dark, buzz-cut hair and a goatee, and he doesn't really look like a kid. He tells me exactly how much better he can make every part of his car and how much money it will cost. He takes Diane everywhere she wants to go and does what she tells him to, like for example picking me up.

We go to Lucky's mother's house, stopping at the top of the long stony driveway between the fields. Carl, I can tell, is dying for a guy to talk to. In the silence I can hear the Camaro sucking air like it's breathing. Then the door is suddenly yanked open and Lucky is standing there. I don't know if he knows I'm coming. Carl doesn't say anything, and the interior lights make the red carpet and leather give off a lurid glow that reminds me of the booth we sat in in Rudi's bar. Lucky hesitates, and the cold air pours in. In the end we just say hi like we've never met before and he squeezes behind me into the back seat.

"You want a beer?" Carl pulls out a six-pack of cans in plastic rings. Lucky says no. Then at the last second Carl asks me, but I say no too. Carl pops one with a loud fizz and casually throws it back, but I can see him feel with his free hand to see how much foam landed on his carpet. Diane meets us at the door in black slacks and a cream sweater. I'm still wearing jeans with dirt marks on the butt from skating in the woods. Everybody's a little uptight, wondering what's going to happen, but we are all excited, even Lucky. Diane sends Carl and Lucky downstairs to pick a movie. She rolls her eyes when Lucky passes by.

"I told you he likes you."

"Diane, he kissed me." Her mouth drops open and her eyes light up like it's the greatest thing in the world. In a way it is, but I don't want to be juvenile about it. "Can we not talk about it now? I don't want to jinx it, okay? You're so dressed up. Is this a party?"

"My parents are out all night. My sister's staying at a friend's. I can't believe that little dork has friends."

"What are we going to do tonight, really?"

"Anything we want, I guess."

She sits down across from me at the kitchen table and looks me in the eyes.

"What do you think about Carl?"

"He's ... he's not like a kid. How old is he, anyway?"

"Sixteen. He's got a full-time job."

"Does your mother give you a hard time about riding in his car?"

"She doesn't know about him at all." Her voice is too low. Her green eyes are holding something back. I'm afraid of hearing it right now. I ask her about her hair, if she's going to Manic Panic the roots, which are coming in brown. She ignores this.

"He loves me. He's like, real – not like all those wise-ass

boys at school."

"More like a man?"

"I love him, Kate. He's a real person, not just a dumb kid. And ..." She looks at me.

"Oh my God. Really?"

"Yes. He adores me, Kate. I can feel it. He thinks of me all the time."

"Oh my God, you make me feel like such a baby!"

I touch her hand. Now we're shy. But she grabs my hand like always. "I feel like it's real, like I'm not just playing pretend shit all the time."

"You are so awesome, Diane."

We go downstairs. Lucky and Carl are playing an old video game they found on a shelf, like they're back in the sixth grade or something.

"Is this like, what we're going to do?" I can't stop myself.

"It's different when you're drinking. Much harder!" Carl is actually the only one drinking, but soon Diane clicks open a beer tab and sips from the can like she's been drinking all her life. I look over at Lucky, but he waves away the beer and keeps playing. I'm not going to drink if he's not. When I sit down next to him on the sofa, he throws the controller aside. We're all sitting around, but it's different from all the hanging around I've ever done. If you're not gaming and you're not drinking and you're not fooling around or watching some show, you have to talk to each other. It's exciting and so cool that Diane and Carl are in love, but it makes me feel like Lucky and I are the baby brother and sister. I don't know anything about Carl and so naturally I start asking him stuff, but it's like he's too shy to talk to me once he's out of his car.

Lucky's never seen Carl before, but he starts asking him all this stuff about his car and his job. Diane throws in some answers for Carl. Carl's parents are divorced and his father lives in Florida. He says his mother nags him, but he has to live there another year because he owes her for the down payment on the car.

"That's it? You'll just move out after you make the last payment?" I know I should let it go, but I can tell Carl is a sweetheart and it's hard to believe his mother is just a loan company to him.

"Yeah, I want to be on my own. I just do the math, and when it adds up to zero I move out."

Lucky asks him more questions about his car and his company and his job and his rent. Lucky's a little like his father, the contractor. Carl has answers for all of this stuff because he's on his own and he must have to think about this a lot. I don't want to grow up and think about all this cold, boring stuff all the time. Diane looks bored too.

"Hey, Carl. Did Diane tell you about Wellness class today? Smokin Suzy's head caught on fire."

"What?"

"Yeah, it's true," Lucky says. "Her head burst into a ball of flame with all this bad-smelling smoke coming off it. Then her face turned black and melted into itself."

"Are you shitting me? Is that true?"

"Yeah. Mrs. Davis woke up and sent the class out into the hall. Johnny Gott was funny. He gets down on his knees in the hall and says, 'God, I promise! I ain't *never* smoking again!'"

While Carl's asking more about Smokin' Suzy, Lucky puts his hand on top of mine. Right away we're two couples again. Diane starts looking at Carl with dreamy eyes. Carl wants to hear more school stories, but Lucky is quiet and I can't think of anything but his hand holding mine and imagining we're alone. Finally, Carl meets Diane's eyes and they seem to float away together up the stairs.

Carl comes back. "Hey, you guys. Check this out." He pulls a beautiful little wooden box out of his jacket pocket. It's all lined inside like you'd expect to see a pearl necklace in it, but there's nothing in it but a little contraption made out of bolts or something. "It's a metal dope pipe. Made it at work."

"Cool!" Lucky holds it up and looks at it like it's a valuable jewel. Maybe it's me, maybe I just don't know how good dope is. "Looks like it's never been used."

"You guys break it in." Carl looks at me too. "You two guys take it. It's a present."

Lucky fiddles with the pipe for a minute, then puts it down, but he doesn't say anything and doesn't take my hand again. I figure maybe we can do normal talk, so I ask him how he got out of his mother's house.

"It was easy. She's not home."

"Today was fun for me. The whole thing. It was a great day."

I guess I'm not the hard-to-get type.

"How did you get out of your house tonight? What did you tell your father?"

"That creepy house. My father's like a ghost now. He didn't even see me."

"When my father split with my mother he went out and got drunk for so long he lost half his business."

"My Dad right now is staring at a wall in the dark. He's been doing that since before I got home. I even tried to, you know, hug him, but he pushed me away. I can't stand it there."

"He loves you, Kate."

"You don't even know him."

"How could he not love you? How could anybody who knows you not love you?"

So, what are you saying, Boy Wonder?

"When you kissed me today, was that just because ...?"

I don't know what I want him to say. My lips, all on their own, are just begging him to kiss them. He does. It's really sweet. Soon the sweetness is everywhere and I'm starting to like melt inside. Then I feel like I'm sort of turning inside out and I don't want to do this in front of him. I grab his wrists and push him away just a little. He looks in my eyes.

"I do like it. I mean, you could tell that, couldn't you?"

He laughs.

"What?"

"No, I thought you liked it. I liked it. A lot."

He lets me lean into him and sort of collapse on his chest. My arms are around him. I can't see his face, so for all I know he's rolling his eyes and thinking when is this weird chick going to get off me? But I don't think so.

"I'm so scared to go back to that house. Dad's turned it so cold and creepy."

"You said before he's still in love with your mother."

"I wish I could help him, but he doesn't even want me around."

"Maybe he's just having a bad night or something."

"You're saying I should just forget about it?"

"No. Yeah. Maybe you should."

"But I have to go back there tonight. You can't imagine what it feels like there."

"Just for now, let's think about right here, right now. I feel really good right now."

"Oh, yeah. This is so the opposite of Dad's house."

"After we dropped you off tonight, when my father and I were alone, I did something I never had the guts to do before. I asked him to get rid of Rudi."

"What did he say?"

"We were in the driveway of his house. He threw his beer bottle in the yard. He just said, 'She's all I have.'"

"What did you say?"

"Nothing. When my father starts a sentence by throwing a beer bottle, it's generally not the time to start a logical argument. Anyway he's pissed at me now, at both her and me."

"I don't like her."

"Join the crowd. But I think he really loves her."

We lie on the carpet, propped up with some pillows. I'm touching his face, examining every line like a wonder of nature, feeling his bristly man-like little whiskers with my fingers, running my hand over his shaved head. He tries to kiss me again, and when I won't let him he pulls my hand off.

"Sorry. About groping your head. You're really so fascinating to me."

"Kate, I'm usually pretty confident things will turn out okay. But right now, I'm absolutely sure of it."

I lean into him and he lets me kiss him so gently.

Then he kisses me softly himself, and this time I'm not delirious. No, I'm not. This is real. Things will be okay. Lucky is not only gorgeous, he is the best person I've ever known. And I can feel in my heart right now, that even if everyone else would disappear at this very instant, Lucky and I could start the world all over again, all by ourselves, right here from this room, right now. And it would be a better world. We have the key, right here, right now.

I want to say that I love him but I'm too embarrassed because his touch is making me squirm and I have to twist away, but I don't want to leave that room and he is so kind, so kind, and I don't really know if I am kind to him because I know I have to do one of two really scary things and I choose the one that is easiest for me but that might hurt him the most.

Chapter 12

Looking through the glass in the door of the teachers'
lounge, I see Mr. Folsom hunched over his coffee, all alone. He's
staring at a picture of the moon landing taped on the wall above
the mini-fridge. My tap on the glass jerks him out of his moon-
coma. I can't believe Dad cut me such a break last night. The day
outside is gorgeous. Kids aren't supposed to be in the teachers'
lounge, but I go in.

"Why the big smile, Kate?"

"Can I talk to you? I was kissing this boy ..."

"Oh." He drops his shaky hands down to the arms of this
chair. "Are you sure I'm the right one to talk to about this?"

"I can't talk to anyone else." He's fidgeting, but I can't stop
myself. "So, there's this boy, and I really like him, and we were
kissing, and I get this feeling, this really nice feeling – don't
interrupt me, please. I'm not totally ignorant. I know it was
some kind of a sex thing."

"Kate, those feelings are perfectly normal."

"Not for me. Not for me. And so I'm wondering, if I'm
feeling this way when I kiss him, is that what people mean, really,
when they say they're in love?"

"Kate, I think it would be a big mistake to confuse sexual
feelings with love."

"What is love?"

He opens his mouth but no words come out, and I can tell

he's really, really sorry we started this.

"I can't say. It's not the same as sex."

His eyes are on me but he isn't really looking. He's somewhere else now. I can tell that he was in love somewhere else, at least once.

"And what I came to ask you, if a person really does love you, and if you're kissing and all, and everything he does brings those great feelings, and if you just do it together, right then – wouldn't that be just the sweetest thing there is? Honestly?"

"I can't talk about this." He's looking away, tapping on the table, looking away at the poster on the wall. There's pain in his face.

"It can be a good thing, Kate."

"A *good thing*?"

He swallows so hard I can see it in his bony neck. He smiles sadly, and it's a vacant smile like he's still someplace far away. But he does come back, and he looks at me this time like he really sees me.

"I won't lie to you, Kate. Walking on the moon is probably a poor second best."

"You were snoring! For Christ's sake, I had to pretend there was something wrong with the phone!"

I had fallen asleep at my desk while Triandos and I were having a telephone conference call with the County Executive.

"I'm sorry."

"I'm sorry, too. Are you really here at all, Sam?" I looked at him, and his annoyance started to fade. "What's the problem, Sam?"

So I had to tell him some of it, and then I told him more than I meant to. Triandos is one of those guys who's always got a bigger problem – more kids, less money, more flak from the county council. Just to keep the Recreation Department from being zeroed out every year, he says, he has to kiss so much ass his lips are sore. But he enjoys his job, his family, his gripes. He's good at it all, and nobody pushes him around very much. He's happy where he is, but he'll be even happier when eight more years have passed and he'll be able to retire.

"Clare caught me last night. She called at 11:15 and I had to admit I didn't know where Kate was. Now she'll use that against me."

"So? What was Clare doing herself that she was too busy to call until 11:15?"

"I couldn't ask her that."

"Why not?"

I looked at him. "Because she'd tell me."

If Triandos was disgusted with me, he hid it well. He sat there and waited, and I had to go on.

"It was my fault," I went on. "Kate was hugging me, you know, too tight, and I pushed her away. I was sitting there in the dark, and I just – I don't know, I didn't want to be reminded of ... anything. I didn't even notice when she left. I went out driving, looking for her everywhere. I couldn't call the police – you know, because of the custody battle. I finally set the alarm for midnight. I don't know what I was going to do at midnight. When the alarm went off, she was in her room, pretending to be asleep, so I pretended to wake her up. Her pupils were dilated, and she went downstairs and ate everything in the kitchen. I'm sure she was smoking pot."

This wasn't the whole truth. Kate was back upstairs and really asleep by one. But I was awake for three hours after that, sitting on the bed in the dark, getting up and staring at the empty street. I ended up thinking about Clare. I was slipping again. At least I recognized it this time, and I had the sense to hide that from Triandos. Maybe that was a step.

Clare was in the room, right there on the desk the whole time I was talking to Triandos. Her voice mail message was in the phone right next to me, and that message was more real to me then than Triandos standing right in front of me in all his shaggy Greek glory. It was a sickness to have saved that voicemail, I knew.

"I'm no psychologist, but it seems to me you screwed up. You like the kid, right?"

"The idea of losing her – I would just die."

"So don't push her away. She just showed you how far away she can get, and how fast."

"Yeah. You're right. I pushed her out, didn't I?"

"Cause and effect." Triandos spread his hands, palms up. I had always liked him. Lately his thick black hair was getting grey around the edges, and he had grown a small paunch that showed under his maroon and grey striped shirt with the silver tie. Cause and effect. Life could be so simple if you weren't nuts. I didn't tell him just how hard Kate and I were hugging each other that night and how in all that sobbing closeness when I was holding her I forgot that she was not Clare.

After Triandos stepped back to his office, I picked up the phone and pressed all the required buttons until I got Clare's message.

"Sam, I'm sorry for yelling at you about Kate. At least you were there when she finally came back. At least she would come home to you. I'm worried about her. I've talked to the principal at her school.

"Sam, dragging this divorce out can't be helping her. Let's get this over with.

"Sam ..." (Three times, my name.) "I don't think I'm being too unreasonable to ask for something. So far, you have everything: the savings, the house, the tract in Alexander's Woods – and you have Kate too, at least so far.

"You're still thinking about Alexander's Woods, and how we were going to build our dream house there. I had that dream too. I admit it was possible once." Her voice was at her softest and kindest. "I know you still think about that, Sam, but you have to face the fact that it's not going to happen. We never had enough money to do it, we didn't have any more kids, and Kate is almost gone now. Holding onto that land is not going to help you hold onto me. You have to face the fact that I'm gone, Sam."

Somewhere in those soft syllables behind that blinking red light was the plain fact that she really did know me once and really did love me once, but now did not love me any more. I could not reconcile the soft voice with the hard facts, the familiar timbre with no-love. If only I could …

I recognized Triandos' shirtsleeve as his arm roughly came over my shoulder and pressed the buttons necessary to delete the message. I jumped back and glared at him.

"You don't want to do that to yourself," he said, unashamed.

"You might not believe this, but I do realize what I'm doing to myself is bad. I am trying to stop. But it's really hard."

"You can't just stop?"

"What I was doing just now … this is just the kind of thing I was doing last night when Kate slipped away."

"I can see that. You gotta stop. For your kid, you gotta stop. Clare's not coming back, Sam. I just heard her say it four times. The bitch isn't coming back."

The truth is awesome. I walk away from the teachers' lounge and can't wait to get outside. There's got to be a reason the sun is so super-bright. I was in such a hurry when I got out of bed this morning I fast-washed and blow-dried my hair and pinned it back in a loose ponytail, and so now all the wild blond frizz is bouncing off my shoulders. Mom says my face is too round for that look, but how smart can she be? She's dating that sleazoid Anton while I am falling in love with Lucky.

The smooth ceramic tiles flash the sunlight back and forth in front of me. Outside, squadrons of giant yellow leaves twirl in the air, bounce onto the walk and skitter noisily along, flattening themselves against my ankles. I see Lucky coming out of the woods at the top of the trail. Suddenly, when we get really close, we get awkward, facing each other with our mouths hanging open. The leaves are batting us in the face like to remind us to say something.

"Thanks for getting me home last night."

"No. It was really cool to see inside your actual house, where you live and all."

So, for sure, it's happening to him too. The leaves are spinning around us and the sky is so blue you can see all the way to space.

"Did you get busted by your Dad?"

"He was so cool with it. It was a good night. It was a really good night."

A clattering metallic noise drowns us out, and a big truck bumps onto the sidewalk and then goes on the grass in front of the school. Lucky frowns in that direction.

"More posthole diggers."

"Why are they tearing down the whole school?"

"If I get detention today, I'll find out why."

Inside, Mr. Folsom looks up when he sees Lucky and I come in together. He's practically staring at me and I'm wondering what's wrong, but then our eyes meet and his smile is so real I just know he knows.

Johnson's guard stands in front of him with a hand on either side of his head, forcing him to look at his desk and not at me. Folsom doesn't call on me the whole class because he knows my math mind will be blank and the moon can wait for another day.

"When you go to high school next year," Ms. Nesbitt's look is even a little more off-kilter than usual, "there will be dances."

Dead quiet.

The genius of Lucky is he can say what everyone is thinking.

"What?"

"Dancing is important. I mean old fashioned dancing. A communication with the opposite sex. An icebreaker." She's got everything, beautiful wild curls, giant brown eyes behind those klutzy thick-framed glasses, a good figure behind those crazy loose dresses, long legs, brains. She can get anyone's attention. But the thing about Ms. Nesbitt is you're never sure she's not going to go flying apart right in front of your eyes.

"So, dancing is sex?" Johnny Gott, of course.

"People learn to dance," Ms. Nesbitt holds out her arms like she's dancing with a partner, "the old fashioned way. You touch," she sways and takes sweeping, dipping steps, "but it is not violent. It is graceful. And there are rules."

"It is so important!" Lucky is the only one who will always go along with Ms. Nesbitt. "Maybe you should teach it to us, outside, right now, before we get to high school and it's all so ... *scary*."

And she does. She takes us all outside, but the class is a disaster. Ms. Nesbitt is one of those teachers who has no idea who's popular or even who's a moron, and she picks Johnny Gott to learn to dance in front of the class with a girl named Margaret Ann. Margaret Ann's a little fat, and Johnny acts so juvenile she won't dance with him. He dances by himself, jerking around, but when he comes close to her again she slaps him in the face.

"No one will dance with me," he complains to the crowd.

"Maybe Fag Folsom will dance with you," someone yells. And then a lot more people yell it.

People stop laughing when they see that Ms. Nesbitt is crying. Things get so quiet everybody notices that Principal Freeland has come out of the school and is trudging his way out toward us. Johnny Gott pulls out a metal chair for Ms. Nesbitt to sit down on, and he sits in the stands facing her like the rest of us.

"We're all going to cover for her," he says, but we don't even have any books or papers or anything.

She pulls herself together as he steps closer.

"Would you like me to explain my lesson plan?" she calls out as he approaches.

Freeland looks at her like he's surprised to see her at all. He keeps walking past her and right into the stands – until he is right in front of me.

"Kate, I want to see you in my office right after your last class."

"Why?" I wish my voice was strong like Ms. Nesbitt's, but it's not.

"Just be there."

This can't be good. Dad told me Mom's been talking to Freeland. I can't focus on the dancing class, and it's over in a few minutes anyway. I worry about this meeting all day, but when I show up Ms. Cascio tells me that Freeland was called out to some emergency meeting with the County Executive, and I'm free to go. I'm walking right down the middle of the hallway very fast, trying to get out of there as quick as I can, but I see the door to Mr. Folsom's classroom open with the light on, and I go in.

"How are you, Kate?" What's so sad about Mr. Folsom is how he tries so hard to be a normal person but will never make it.

"Okay. Actually, really great today."

"Lucky's the one, isn't he?"

I don't want to say, so I look down. Of course he can tell by the look on my face.

"I was wondering how you stand it, trying to teach math every day to so many ninth-grade nutbrains and jerkoffs."

"A lot of kids make important choices at this age, go one way or another."

"But they are such jerks! How do you stand it?"

"I thought you were happy today."

"I am. Happy for me. But ... okay, a bunch of kids in Ms. Nesbitt's class today were calling you 'Folsom the Fag.'"

His face twists up, in pain I guess, or maybe he's trying to make a lie come out.

"Everybody knows it," I say. "And I want to ask you about it."

His face goes pale like he never wants to trust anyone with the true story of his real life, but his eyes are right on mine.

"You know what you said to me this morning, about going to the moon being a poor second best?" I say. "I know that's true. I can tell already."

"That's wonderful, Kate."

"But will *you* ever be happy like that?"

"Being gay doesn't mean that you can't love, in every way."

"But you're a teacher."

I had no idea until yesterday how important this all was. I thought until yesterday that it was just a kind of game we all played until whoever we happened to be with at a certain age was the one we married.

"Has it ever hit you really hard? You know, where you can't think of anything else?"

He snorts a short laugh.

"But you're gay, and you're a teacher. You can never – there must be almost nobody ..."

"Almost nobody. You're right. It's like that for a lot of people, Kate."

"Then why do you give a fuck about the moon? If there's nobody ..."

"*Almost* nobody, Kate. It's the *almost* that counts. It only takes one, if it's the right one."

Chapter 13 &

"Can you at least understand how I'm having trouble letting go?"

Clare and I were in Collier's, a quiet, musty restaurant in Glenwood that looked from the outside like the old Victorian house it once was. Glenwood is small enough that the owner recognized us, and large enough that he didn't know that we were separated. Clare wore her prettiest office dress, a short, shimmery green number that she bought for closings. Our table was in one of the many small rooms that made up the restaurant. There was a long window with intricate moldings and ruffled curtains looking out over the wooden porch. The carpet was thick enough to quiet the voices at the other two tables nearby.

I found the courage to tell her straight out how much I missed her. As we talked, I watched her and listened carefully to every word she said for a sign that she was having second thoughts. She spoke respectfully to me then, but without a trace of regret. When she called for the check I ordered a second round of drinks and a dessert that neither of us touched.

"I didn't know this would be so painful for you," she admitted, sipping on the coffee that I had practically forced her to order.

"You mean, right now? Having dinner with you?"

"Oh. Is even this dinner a problem?"

"It is. You look so beautiful tonight."

"Stop it, Sam. I thought you wanted to meet to get this business settled."

"Not business. It's not business to me. I love you."

She did look into my eyes at that point.

"Sam, it's not even the real me that you want. You just want some crazy idea of me that you have. I tried to be like your idea of me, Sam. It drove me crazy. Didn't you notice I was out of the house working ten hours a day long before I even met Anton?"

"It was real. You did love me once."

She gathered up her purse and stood up. "Don't do this to me, Sam." She looked really sad, though she wouldn't let me catch her eye as she quickly picked up the rest of her things. She stepped away from the table. I felt that I could not just sit there and let it all end like that. I threw money on the tablecloth and ran out after her.

I caught up to her in the parking lot. Yes, I put my weight against her car door when she tried to open it.

"Don't do this to me. Please, just let me get in my car and leave."

"Please, Clare. We've been married for sixteen years. Let me have one last minute."

She sobbed softly, then nodded. A rush of hope shot through me as I sat in the car next to her.

There are things that, even as you are saying them, you know will never work.

"Please, please don't go. Everything I ever did was for you. I tried to be everything you wanted me to be. I can see now, that must have been so boring to you. You wanted more of a man."

"Sam ..."

"Please let me finish. I think I can change. I think I can do better. It's possible you could love me again."

"Sam." She looked out through the windshield, where we could see a group of diners walking toward their car, which was right next to us. Then she looked down, then she looked over at me. There were tears in her eyes. "You can't live just for me."

"How about if I live for just you and Kate?"

She smiled sadly. "You love her so much. And you can talk to her. You never would talk to me, except for jokes. I got tired of those jokes, Sam."

"I'll get new material."

"Sam, listen to me. I am in love with Anton."

"You said you would love me forever."

"I know what I said, but that was a long time ago, Sam, and it was – *situational*. Sam, please look at me."

She brushed her fingers against my downcast chin and gently coaxed my face up towards hers. Then she kissed me.

It felt like the real thing, so warm that I responded, waves of feeling welling up inside me as our lips touched. I put my lips to her ear and whispered things I shouldn't have. She pushed me back gently and said oh Sam and kissed me again. It was a straight-on, warm kiss, but I knew it was a present. And I knew this was our last kiss. In a way it was sweeter because of this, because it was never going to happen again. I knew she didn't feel that kiss the same as I did. Her love for me now was a patronizing thing. She felt that she knew me totally, and she didn't want anything at all from me any more. She was giving me something; that was all.

She rested her head on my shoulder, giving me what she knew I wanted because I had told her how badly I suffered. I felt small to be accepting this gift, but I accepted it anyway. A trace of perfume coming through the forest of her hair diminished me further. I was lost in her again, and not above begging.

After she had sped out of the parking lot, I sat in my own car and cried. I just bawled, sobbing over what I thought we had been to each other, and how it was gone, so totally gone. What was humiliating was the price I had paid for that last kiss. I had thought she wanted to know how I felt, so I had told her about my depression, and how I had held Kate too tight and then pushed Kate away until she slipped away, maybe for good. I told her Kate smoked pot that night. I told her that I wanted Alexander's Woods because I inherited them from my mother and they were the only things I knew were really mine and because letting Anton have them would destroy my last shred of self-respect. I told her that I would give her the whole house instead as soon as Kate went away to college.

I told her everything because I thought she had some interest in me, but by the time she drove away I knew better. I cried until the tears wouldn't come any more, and then I sat there longer, drying my eyes on my shirt sleeve until the busboys came out of the side door of the restaurant and lit cigarettes in the parking lot. One of them left the group; I could see by tracking the tiny red glow of his cigarette that he was walking toward my car, probably wondering why I was still sitting there a half hour after the restaurant had closed. I started the engine quickly. I had no choice but to move on.

Chapter 14

Mr. Folsom hands me a note.

"From the office. Principal wants to see you this afternoon right after classes."

"What does he want?"

"I don't know. I told him you were doing really well in algebra. I gave you the benefit of the doubt on that, Kate. He said he missed meeting with you yesterday and it absolutely has to happen today."

"Is my mother going to be there?"

He shrugs. What I really want is for him to volunteer to come with me, but he's way too afraid of Freeland for that to happen.

Freeland pokes his head into the outer office and waves me into his inner one.

"You were out on the streets until midnight the night before last."

"I know you talk to my mother."

"You were smoking pot."

Who else is he talking to?

"Who gave you pot?"

What can they do to me, really, for smoking pot once? I don't say anything, and he stares at me.

"You're fortunate that you're not on probation."

"I'm not on probation."

"Your friend, Lucky, though, that's another story. If he had his urine tested, and it came up positive for marijuana, he could be put away."

Lucky and I were kissing, lying on the sofa in the basement of Diane's house, and everything was so sweet. I was dying just to melt into him. But I got scared when he touched me and I jumped up, and then – I didn't mean to – I started giggling. He chased me around the room until we both fell back on the sofa again, his arms strong around me. He wanted to kiss me again but I was afraid. I knew what would happen. I wanted to do something really special with him right then, but not that. So I said let's try out Carl's dope pipe. I could see in his face that he really didn't want to, but I held his wrists with my hands and reminded him that he said we were so safe, the two of us alone here in this room, this night. Let's make the two of us, alone here in this room, last for a thousand years. I said that.

"I can pick up that phone and have Lucky picked up and tested."

This is all my fault. Lucky lit the little pipe and showed me how to smoke it. I burned my fingers and coughed a lot at first, but suddenly there was no such thing as time and Lucky and I were alone forever in that sacred place. He still tried to kiss me but it was more like a game. We were running around and throwing pillows and stuff and laughing. Then he caught me and held me down on the carpet. I was lost in his eyes, helpless. He kissed me, just once.

"I've never done this before."

"I've done it three or four times. The first time, it seems like you've discovered eternity, but after a while you get used to it and dope's not that great."

"No, I meant that I never really kissed a boy before."

He didn't say anything.

"What? Could you tell?"

"I heard girls practice kissing on oranges."

I hit him with a pillow.

"I know your parents are fighting over Alexander's Woods. Why doesn't your father just give up the woods so he can have the house and keep custody of you?"

Through the window behind Mr. Freeland's desk, I can just see the edge of the soccer stands. I have a good view of a big machine dumping dirt into a truck right near the entrance to the path that goes through Alexander's Woods.

"There's not really any hope that your mother and father are ever going to get back together again."

Even if it's true, I know he shouldn't be saying it. Nobody who is a good person would say that.

"So why won't your father give your mother Alexander's Woods?"

"I don't know. I don't care."

"But you should care about it, Kate. You should care about it a lot."

"Why should I care?"

"Those woods. They are not only important to your mother, Kate. They are important to me."

"They're not important to me."

"Lucky is important to you."

He's smiling like a wolf showing his teeth before he bites.

"What's important to you is that Lucky not get tested for pot right now."

Freeland leans toward me and shows me his real face, his wolf face.

"I can have Lucky picked up and tested. We both know the test will show positive for marijuana. He'll be put away. You don't know what it's like in there, Kate. It's not a nice place. It will be so hard in there, and he'll be in there for so long, he won't be the same person when he gets out."

"Please don't do that!"

"It's going to happen, and only one thing can stop it from happening. It's going to happen unless your father agrees to give up Alexander's Woods. Today."

Chapter 15

Freeland makes me sit there like I'm his prey. The sharp sun coming in sideways through the window deepens the hard lines in his face. I have been bad to my friend. I am bad, and Freeland knows I am weak and he can make me do even much worse.

"So," he says, "are you going to make it happen?"

My knees are wobbling when I stand up. He gets up too and comes around the desk at me, but it's not me any more but a scared animal whose hands fly up so he can't hit me. The look on his face changes and he stops and actually backs away a little, and just then I get the strength to run out. I'm moving fast on the jittery high of escape when I turn the corner and practically crash into Johnson.

"Kate!"

His deep brown eyes catch and hold mine, draw me in.

"Kate," he pleads in a whisper, "I love you."

I knock his hands away. I run outside, hitting the big red door so fast it slams hard behind me. I run alongside the fence at the edge of the soccer field towards the woods. I'm breathing hard, but calm inside. All the colors are sharp and vivid and clear. An archway of yellow leaves floats over the entrance to the path. Lucky always glides through these woods like he was born here. He says people aren't improving things by ripping down woods and putting up schools and houses and filling them up with people. I say it all depends on who the people are.

I hear the metal school door clank behind me again. Johnson is on the loose, stumbling and limping down the sidewalk toward me. But I'm way ahead of him, and when I look back, he's just a little black speck, moving very slowly, losing ground. I guess he does love me, if there is a kind of love that wants to grab you and beat you and claw you.

Tangles of brown honeysuckle vines strangle the pure green meadow. You can still hear a few bugs screeching. The squirrels make a big racket rattling through the dry brush. There are still huge clumps of giant sparkling grass, all flattened now.

Lucky and I thought that nothing we did together in that room could be wrong. It felt so safe once we knew we loved each other. We had to consecrate that room. There were only two choices, one that put him in danger and one that was really scary to me. To be perfectly honest, I'm still not sure I made the wrong choice, but I wonder if that would be the choice of someone who is a good person and who is really in love.

Black rocks spotted with green moss stick out of the high bank on one side of the trail. A bush arches its branches of tiny amber leaves up high so the sun shines through them. There are weird bird sounds high in the trees, like ducks quacking. Why are none of us as beautiful as the world we can see right in front of us? I cross the bridge and keep on the trail all the way to Lucky's mother's house.

Lucky's mother has dark hair like his, but she goes for the straight and sculpted instead of the shaved head look. She's wearing a dark blue women's business suit over a starched white blouse, and small gold earrings. The whole outfit's one step up from what Mom wears in doing whatever business she does with Anton. She seems too sophisticated for this old country house. She smiles at me now, but I know that she'll hate me soon as this slut who drugged up her only son.

"Can I see Lucky?"

"And who is this?"

She almost sings it, with a smile. So I know I'm not yet dirt in her eyes.

"I'm Kate, his friend. We're in class together."

"You've been running."

"I don't like to go through the woods alone."

"Well, Lucky's not here. And he's supposed to be. Ralph, his stepfather, is supposed to keep track of him, but he had to work late and he's not here either. You can wait for him inside, if you'd like."

"I don't think so. Just ask him to call me if you see him."

She nods and shuts the door like she's already thinking about something else. Lucky must be at his father's house, and so I have to go back through the woods. I'm not afraid of Johnson here in the woods, but I pick up a big stick anyway. So many leaves have fallen from the black skeletons of the trees that the weak twilight glows all the way down to the forest floor.

I hear a whining sound ahead of me on the path, just around a curve. It's awful, like maybe a small animal is being tortured. I kneel down to hide behind the smooth trunk of an old fallen tree like a small animal myself. The sound is louder and now more like a moaning, and almost human. Somebody is being hurt over and over. When the moaning stops for a second, I try to catch my breath. Then I hear a voice calling my name.

I have to keep going ahead, my legs wobbling, from tree to tree. I'm holding onto the last tree, and not looking, when my stomach starts to turn and I know what I am going to see. It's Johnson on the bridge, his naked flesh standing out pinkish-yellow against the sleeping colors of the forest. He's sitting, facing away from me with his legs dangling toward the stream, looking up into the air, rhythmically calling my name. His moans are in synch with his hand. My name is in synch with his hand.

When I come to the bridge, he sees me and is ashamed – I can see him blush all over – but he keeps moaning my name and pumping away because he can't stop himself. I can't stand to be inside of him like that. Holding the stick, I run behind him across the bridge and tell myself I will never see him again.

"Kate."

"Keep away from me!"

I stop and try to look just at those pleading brown eyes. He's still doing it while trying to talk to me now. Then the eyes go blank and he gasps. I just want to throw up. I can't control what I do next. He has gotten to me, inside of me somehow. Then I'm running on pure fear, crashing through the woods to Lucky's father's house.

All the way there I'm sure he's trying to follow me. Rudi's little brown car is at the very end of the driveway, but it zooms away with a trail of dust behind it. I'm still scared, even inside the fence. The house looks empty. I run over to the place where Lucky's father keeps his gun, but just as I touch the roof of the birdhouse and start to swing it open, something slams into me from behind.

Molson is hysterical, running around in a blur of purplish-brown fur. He's licking my face, jumping up on me when I try to stand up, and running around me in nervous circles. He runs back and forth between me and the deck.

He guides me through the birdhouses and the weather vanes and wagon wheels and other junk. Duke doesn't even get up from her spot on the deck. Potted plants are hanging in macramé nets from wooden beams over the deck. Lucky told me his father built this thing. The beams are so thick they look like they could hold up the Titanic. Molson is so happy, but as soon as I put my foot on the lowest step leading to the deck, he growls at me.

"What's the matter, Molson?" I try to talk to him like Lucky would. I don't know much about dogs. Then I see it. Duke is lying on her side on a big, flattened-out cardboard box, and there's a whole pile of tiny puppies snuggled up next to her. Duke is licking them. Their eyes are closed and they keep squirming all over each other – trying to get at her nipples, I guess. Molson is still prancing around, definitely the proud, nervous father.

I step over as slow and soft as I can, but when I crouch down close to the puppies she growls at me. Molson starts barking, not like he is really mad at me but like it's his job or something, so I back off. No lights are on in the house.

There is a porch in front of the house, and I guess some day Lucky's father is going to put steps up to it. There's a big window on the driveway side of the house with a huge square flowerpot underneath. I stand on the flowerpot and look in the window. The living room is empty, with a light shining through the door that goes to Rudi's room, but nobody answers when I yell in.

There's a crunching sound of tires on the driveway behind me.

"Kate, Kate!" Lucky's father's voice drowns out the noise of his dying truck engine. By the time I turn around, he's bounced out of the truck and is coming toward me.

"I was looking for Lucky."

"Ain't seen him. You check at his mother's house?"

"He's not there."

"You seen the puppies yet?" Earl is as excited as Molson.

"Oh yeah. They're so cute. Duke won't let me near them."

"They'll let you get close, if they trust you."

He's on the porch, squatting down in his dusty jeans, ruffling Duke's fur and calming her with his deep voice. Molson comes over and tries to lick his face just as he reaches for one of the puppies. Most of them are all black like their mother. Lucky's father eases his hand closer and sneaks a puppy away from Duke's belly, and then hands it over to me like I would know what to do with it. This one is reddish brown, like Molson. Actually, I do just naturally know what to do with it. I hold him in one hand and stroke his fur with one finger. He is so tiny, and his head is hollow and light like a ping pong ball under loose, silky skin.

"Look. He's sleeping right here in my hand."

Earl's craggy face breaks out into a smile.

"Isn't it too cold out here for them?" I ask.

"Oh. Me and Rudi drag them all, box and all, into the kitchen at night. Molson has to go in there with them too, guarding them from ... who knows what." He laughs and slaps Molson affectionately. Molson tries to lick his face again. These sweet creatures are easy to like.

"Do you have any idea where Lucky is?"

His face is creased, I guess from so much working in the sun, but he has Lucky's lively dark eyes. He hears the edge in my voice and looks up.

"You in some kind of trouble, Kate?"

"No."

"But ...?"

"Lucky might be."

"OK. You need to find him. I'll take you to Lucky's mother's."

"He's not there. I've been there."

"He might be there by now. We'll start there again – unless we hear that .357 Magnum go off up the hill in the next five minutes. Don't worry, honey."

"Before we go," he says, turning toward the dogs, " ... what I came for." He searches in the box and pulls out a black puppy who has been at the side, away from all the others, in a corner of the box. He holds it out in two hands for me to see.

"Oh. It's even tinier."

"Yeah. The runt of the litter? You know what that means?"

"The smallest one?"

He reaches over and pours the black puppy into my hands right next to the reddish one. The red one starts squiggling.

"It means the bigger ones can push it away from the mother. Sometimes the runts don't get enough. Sometimes the mother pushes it away herself."

"Did Duke do that?"

"No. But she don't seem to notice he's not getting any."

"So, what are you going to do?"

"You can feed him from a bottle like a baby. An eyedropper, if you have to."

"You?"

"That's where I'm going. One of the guys that works for me, he wants it. Says his wife is home all afternoon. They can feed it every couple of hours." He stands up and claps himself on the forehead. "Afternoon? I just figured it out. That means he's going to skip out on me at least once every morning himself."

I don't want to be standing there while Lucky's Dad talks to his ex-wife, but she comes out at our knock and I'm trapped on the porch with them.

"Is something wrong? Sometimes he plays in the woods until dinner, or he goes over to a friend's house."

"You don't know where he is?"

"I usually have Ralph here to keep track of him from the minute he's out of school. This is the first time Ralph hasn't shown up. Earl," her voice is lower, "I hope you're not going to give me a lot of trouble over Lucky being late this one time."

"No, no, no, no , no. I just met up with Kate here, and she was looking for him."

"Do you want to wait for him here for a while?"

Earl looks at her. "Maybe we'll wait out on the porch. Come on out and talk with us."

I really don't want to be here while they talk to each other, for maybe the first time since they split up.

"I'm going down to check out the puppies in the truck."

I cross the porch and let the old wooden screen door slap shut behind me, but as I start to go down those steps I think of Johnson down there in those woods, in the dark. I wonder if he's out there and if he'll come after me. So I just sit down on the bottom step of the porch. Then, behind me, I can hear them sit down on the crackly wicker chairs.

"Helen, how have you been?" I can hear Earl lean forward in his chair. The long silence after he asks this makes it seem like a really awesome question.

"Fine, Earl. I had my first trial last week. Made a fool of myself at one point. They say it happens to the best of them at first."

"Did you win?"

"Actually, Earl, well, yeah, we did win, pretty much."

"Can't beat winning." There is a longer silence then. I stare at the flower box pushed against the screen. It's filled with stalky petunias waving in the September breeze.

"It was important for me," she says, "to get that degree."

His chair crackles.

"You don't believe that?"

"I can see it now, Helen. You know, for me, everything comes easy. Whatever don't come easy, I just sort of let it slide away."

The chairs don't even crackle. I can hear the petunia stalks scraping against the screen.

"You let a lot slide." I can hear every breath.

"I thought ..." His voice is deep and gravelly, and flat like it doesn't make any difference any more. "I thought it was something simple. You wanted another kind of man."

Petunias scraping.

"That was an easy thing, the easy way for me to think." His voice fills all the space on the porch. It sounds like this is the first time he's really thought about this.

Some sound. A sigh?

"I never did understand the way you thought, Earl. I don't think I have any duty to make an effort now."

I hate to be mean but I have to, is what she's saying. I never heard that kind of talk before, but now I hear it all the time. Then, more softly, she says: "Earl, I thought you would be a better father to Lucky after we split up."

122

"I thought you would let him stay with me sometimes."

"But, Earl, how can I let him be there with that ... woman? She smoked pot with him."

"I told her I'd kick her ass out if she does that again."

"Earl, it's none of my business, but I'm surprised that you ... She's a barmaid, Earl, and she's probably – what, ten years younger than you?"

Then we all hear Ralph's car pull into the drive below. I try to sneak off the steps then, but Earl stands up and opens the screen door and sees me right below him. He looks at me like we've both been hearing things we shouldn't, and he gives me this sad little shrug.

He drives me to my own house, but nobody's there either, and we sit there for a minute with the motor still running. It is starting to get dark, and the puppies in the box are wriggling around. The red one tries to suck on my finger.

"Kate, this red one here's yours if you want it."

"Really? Just ... take it home?" The little red guy was already asleep again. "You mean now?"

"As soon as it's weaned off its mother. In a month or so."

The red puppy nestles against me like I already am its mother. His eyes aren't even open yet and so he thinks having a mother is always a good thing.

Chapter 16 ✎

"Twenty years of this hokey-jokey job, and I've never heard anything like this."

Triandos was standing in my office doorway. It was during that last half hour before we closed up the office, during that quiet time after all the politicians and citizens stop calling, and we finally get a chance to get work done. Triandos had been on the phone in his office with the door closed. The partitions were so thin that I could have eavesdropped on this conversation – as I've sometimes done in the past. It was one of the few fringe benefits of my job as Recreation Administrator II. But right then I was working hard on our annual report to the county council.

He walked in uninvited and draped himself across the chair facing my desk. He pushed it back against the flimsy paneled wall of my office and crossed his legs, ankle over knee, his grey-green suit pants pulled up and showing dark green ribbed socks flowing into black wingtips. He sat still like he had all the time in the world. Triandos had dark eyes and thick black eyebrows peppered with grey. In the eight years we'd been working together, I'd never seen his eyes so wide with interest in me.

"I had no idea," he said, "that things were so bad for you. About your wife, I mean."

"Oh. No, it's nothing. Don't worry about it. It'll go away."

"I say things to you sometimes. Get rid of her. Good riddance. I don't know what I'm talking about. Nothing that bad has ever happened to me. I don't know what I'd do if Betty left. I never even thought about it until this happened to you."

He shifted in his chair, switched ankles and knees.

"Listen to this," he started again. "You know I've been Director of Recreation and Parks for the county for eight years. You've seen me work my ass off, spend five years at night school for that masters degree, and in the last two years apply for every job in the county government that paid a nickel more. At first I was sure I could handle a bigger job. Then, when nothing happened, I thought, maybe not."

"All you've talked about in the last few months is retiring."

"I guess I figured I didn't have what it takes – chutzpah, moxie, political connections, whatever. But today I just got this call from the County Exec." His eyes focused even higher up on the wall, and he shook his head. "And he's talking to me suddenly like he's my oldest friend. He mentions that he may soon need a new man to run the Department of Economic Development. Double my salary. Executive pension after five years."

"Oh, Triandos, that's great! You'd be great at that ..."

"No. Sit down. That's not all. The Exec is even hinting that maybe you could have my job."

"What! How would he even know my name?"

Triandos shrugged, raised his thick eyebrows quizzically.

"It's not a straight deal. Never is. There's always a *quid pro quo*."

"Yeah?"

"We both get the jobs," he said, "on one condition. The condition is that you sell your wife some land called Alexander's Woods. Now, what the hell is that all about?"

The twilight had long since faded by the time Triandos and I were finishing up our talk.

"Let me get this straight. The land is too steep and too small a plot for development. It's zoned residential-forest buffer. It's worth maybe $175,000 at the most. And she's offering you $425,000 for it?"

"Yeah. Actually, her boyfriend, Anton, will pay for it."

"Anton. Oh. Oh, now I see."

"You do?"

"Oh. Oh yeah. Think about it. The County Executive's in on the deal too. What does he have control over? Zoning. What does Anton need to turn a piece of hilly forest into a profitable commercial development?"

"Zoning? But it's a small piece of land."

"What does it border on?"

"Just the school. Oh my God, that reminds me! I've got to get home to Kate."

Triandos didn't move from his chair while I packed up my files and grabbed for my jacket. I stopped and met his eyes.

"I've learned so much over the years from you."

"But," he said, "there's another part of this thing I don't understand at all."

"What?"

"I think we're getting an idea why your wife and Anton and the County Exec want to buy that land. That's no mystery. The real mystery to me is why you don't want to sell it."

Triandos was tough on those employees – and there were a lot of them in the county – who think that county employment does not actually require work, but he had always been friendly to me. I did try to accomplish at least a little something every day. But it was a sad commentary on our department that I was one of his best employees.

Now his big, dog-brown eyes with that keen intelligence focused on me, for the first time ever, not as an employee but as a friend. I felt drawn in by the gentle curiosity in those eyes. So I sat down and told him everything, about our dream house, about how my throat closes up whenever I drive by those woods, how I pray for/dread hearing Clare's voice every time I hear the phone ring.

"My mother gave me those woods. Everything else she had, even her house, went to pay her medical bills. She was the sweetest, kindest person that ever lived. She wanted me to have those woods, and I can't stand the idea of Anton tearing them down just to make money. I'm bad off enough now. If I have to sell them and drive by and see Anton's housing development being built there every day, I'm afraid I might totally snap."

I lowered my eyes and waited, giving him a chance to say something – offer me a couple of Prozac, whatever. Maybe he was waiting for my common business sense to kick in. Was that look in his eyes just disappointment, or was it something else?

"So," I asked, "do I have to sell? I mean, are those my choices, sell or fight with you?"

Waiting for his answer, I glanced out the window, and a thought suddenly jolted me to my feet. It was completely dark outside. I had forgotten Kate again. Triandos didn't move out of the chair, and he kept looking at me. He tapped a shoe with one hand while he glanced around.

"What is it?" I said. "I'm a disappointment to you? You've carried me all these years, and now I'm not willing to help put you over the top?"

"If you did fight against me," his fingers were still tapping, "who would be on your side?"

"No one."

"So Anton and your wife and now the County Exec are all against you. No one's on your side, and now they want me to pile on too. I got to tell you something, Sam. I just can't be part of a fight like that."

Earl drives back to his house with his window open while the heater is blowing down at my feet. Both of the puppies are asleep again in the box on my lap.

Rudi's car is there in the driveway to his house.

"Okay, he's got to be here. Let's go drop off that black puppy first, then come back."

"Can't I get out here now?"

"Don't you want to see how to get set up for a puppy and all?"

"I don't want to be a mother."

"What?"

"I probably can't take care of it."

"You can, honey. Oh. I see. You're at that age when you want to run free yourself."

"Yeah. I guess."

"No problem. Lots of people asked me for these puppies already. Must be that purebred registered bloodline of Molson and Duke."

He laughs at his own joke and winks as I reach for the door handle.

"Tell Rudi I'll be back in ten minutes."

He glides the truck out of the driveway like he doesn't want to wake the puppies. Rudi's brown Nissan has a pink tassel tied to the top of the antenna. I walk down the side of the house past the square yellow glow of the living room window.

There's a yelp like maybe one of the puppies was stepped on, but it's coming from inside the house. I stand up on the flower box and look in that window, but I can't see anything. Then I hear the back door slam. I run to the back just in time to see Lucky leap off the back deck and land in with the dogs, who bark like crazy. Lucky pushes through them and disappears into the darkness before the screen door even hisses shut. I hear him going over the fence.

The floodlight on the back porch snaps on. I duck down behind some big pots of flowers. The door crashes open again and Rudi walks out fast, buttoning her blouse higher against the cold. She calls after Lucky, but he's far gone in the darkness, and she stops at the edge of the deck. She's barefoot and wearing tight jeans and a yellow blouse. She doesn't notice me because she's staring at the spot where Lucky disappeared. The dogs push against her and she ruffles their fur as she stares into the yard. She doesn't go back in for a long time.

Then the floodlights snap off and everything goes black except the moon. Molson comes over and nuzzles me, and I pull him against me like we're giving each other courage. When my eyes get used to the dark, and I can see the yard again, I know what I have to do.

Molson follows me to that birdhouse where they keep the gun. Johnson could still be in those woods, and he really must hate me now. I feel around, sliding my fingers all around inside against the rough wooden boards. But the gun isn't there. I'll have to go without it. I know I should find a way to take Molson with me, but there isn't enough time to figure that all out. So I stumble up the hill, ducking under the low branches of the trees. At the top of the hill, out of breath, I get ready to call out for him.

"Kate."

I almost jump out of my skin. Lucky is leaning back against a tree, facing away from the house. I can't see him that well, but I can hear his breathing.

"You shouldn't follow me. You should keep away from me."

"I have to talk to you."

He doesn't move, and so I just stand there and catch my breath.

"I love you, Lucky."

Nothing. Good.

"I never meant to hurt you. That's the last thing I ever wanted. But ..."

"You don't know me, Kate."

The voice is flat and a little scary in the dark. He seems sadder than I've ever seen him before.

"You're the only one I can talk to."

"No. If you only knew how bad ..." He seems to be part of this dark forest, with sharp black shadows cutting into white glow of his skin. Then I see he's crying, wiping his face on his sleeve.

"Listen."

A couple of thousand years go by. I wipe his tears with my hand.

"I did something," he says, "with Rudi. Something really bad. Not just smoking pot. I can't say it."

I see Rudi again padding out onto the deck a few minutes before, buttoning up her blouse. I see her standing in front of him the other day wearing nothing but a man's shirt and panties, slowly drying her shimmering hair.

"Oh God, I'm going to puke!"

When I say that he runs away, crashing deeper into the woods. I run after him, so close behind him the bushes back-slap me in the face. Just when I get really close, a low branch cuts my ankle out from under me and I fall flat and hard.

"Lucky!"

When he comes back, I grab his hand with both of mine.

"I did something worse, to you."

"Kate, you were the best friend I ever had. I just wish I had met you before. I was already ruined by the time we met."

"Do you love her?"

"I hate her."

The stream was burbling somewhere nearby in the darkness.

"What happened?"

He looks at me, sorry again but still strong. He will always be strong, with or without me. It seems like he's part of nature itself. You can cut it down, but it somehow always grows back.

"She caught me one day looking at some magazines. She grabbed them out of my hands and took them in her room. She thought it was so funny, she said she couldn't wait to tell my father. I was afraid of that. She wouldn't come out of her room, so I went in. She was lying on her bed with nothing on but some tiny see-through stuff. She grabbed my wrist and smacked it and said I was one of those bad boys who look at dirty pictures and now I broke into a real woman's room and was looking at her naked in bed. She smacked me again, but she wouldn't let go of my hand. She said dirty bad boys like me are dying to know what a real woman feels like."

"You did it?"

He nods. "Now when she gets mad at me she says she'll tell my Dad what I did. He loves her so much, Kate, he'll kill me. Me or her.

"Today she was touching me again, I don't know accidentally or what, and she had me just ... so hot I couldn't think about anything else. She told me not to leave the house or she'd tell everyone about what happened before. I ran out anyway. Now I can never go back there."

What kind of creature is he? The nature he worships is so slimy and dangerous. I have to get out of here, get away from him, get out of these woods. My ankle hurts with every step. Johnson is still out here somewhere, looking for revenge on me. I don't even want to touch Lucky, but I have to lean on him to get out of the woods.

The ice-cold water in the stream feels good on the burning cut on my ankle. Lucky goes ahead to check out the bridge, for Johnson. On the way back up the trail, my ankle starts burning again and I have to put my arm up over the back of Lucky's neck. The trail seems longer and darker than ever.

"Lucky, I just thought about something about Rudi."

"What?"

"She's twenty-six. You're fourteen. She'll never tell. She would go to jail."

By the time Lucky says anything, we've limped halfway up

131

the trail toward the school.

"You're right. My mother would definitely put her in jail."

"What she did was wrong."

"We both did it."

What does he want me to say? I'm not saying anything.

"But you're right. She can't tell! So I guess I can still at least go back to my mother's house." He actually laughs. All the time we are talking he keeps patiently dragging me up the path. "Kate, you're so right. Rudi can never tell."

We stop at the edge of the woods, just short of the super-bright lights of the school grounds. Rudi can't tell on him, okay – but what else? The soccer field is like bright green geometry, wet with dew and surrounded by the perfect oval of the track. The aluminum stands on each side lean forward like they're waiting for something to happen. The perfect curves and lines of the baseball field seem ready for kids to come out and play. The bricks of the school are a warm brownish yellow – all set up nice for something good to happen inside. It all makes me so sad – not just for Lucky and me but for all the kids. You can just look at this scene and know that somebody did care, somebody did want things to work. It's supposed to work, but it doesn't. Where are the people who built this for us? Why did they set this all up and then just leave?

"You know," Lucky says, "if she did tell, my father would shoot her."

And I thought this family from the woods would save me.

"Kate, she ... laughed at me, the way that I did it."

"Don't tell me any more about it."

He brought me out of the woods, and I trust him to get me home. And no matter what kind of person he is, I owe him something. He carries me off the path and lays me down in a bed of high mint stalks. He pulls my ankle over his legs and rolls down my sock to take a look at the cut on my foot. The gash isn't nearly as bad as it feels. Lucky strips a few of the long, thin leaves from a nearby stalk and puts them on the cut on my ankle. The leaves are cool and wet with dew. He wrings my sock out and puts it back on over the mint bandage and puts my shoe back on.

"It does feel better."

"An old Indian trick."

"Really?"

"Naw. I saw it on the internet."

"Lucky, I have to tell you something."

"I know. I know. I'm not the guy you thought I was. I swear, Kate, I would have been a better person if only I'd met you a few months earlier."

"Listen. Just listen. I don't think you can even go to your mother's. Freeland found out we were smoking pot. He's going to have you picked up and tested for drugs the minute you get to your mother's house. Lucky, it's my fault, and I can't change it now. I'm really, really sorry."

"Guess I'm running out of homes."

"It was my fault. I begged you to do it."

"Wait a minute. One thing I never heard of is Principal Freeland giving a shit what any kid is doing outside of school. That guy doesn't act like a principal at all. You know the ladies in the office all hate him. They say he was sent here by the big shots just to do some dirty work."

"Lucky, Freeland told me today that I have to make my father give the woods to my mother. He really means it."

"Freeland wants ...? Oh, I get it."

"What?"

"Your mother's in tight with Anton, right?"

"What are you talking about?"

"Remember the night that deer came out right next to us near the driveway? Then it jumped back into the woods when it saw us? Anton's going to clear-cut everything there and scrape it level. Then he'll exterminate every life form that can't pay him

money for the right to be there. You, and me, and your father –
we're just some of those other life forms."

Just then we hear the crack of a gunshot not far down the
trail.

Chapter 17

Lucky pulls me down and tells me not to move. The woods are deathly still, like every plant and creature knows that something horrible has happened.

"Hide your face. Don't even look up."

The lights from the school shine on us through those stalky weeds. At first it's all quiet, except I can hear in my head the sound of my own racing pulse. But then the sound gets louder. Gradually it hits me that the sound is the footsteps of somebody running up out of the woods towards us.

"Keep your face down. Hide your hands. We don't want anything white showing."

We try to shrink down into the ground as the steps come louder and closer. The runner's almost up to us. I can hear him gasping for air as his feet slap the ground like he's staggering. We are frozen on the ground, trying to make ourselves invisible. I'm terrified that those footsteps will come to a stop. I imagine they're slowing down, and he sees us. I'm still holding my breath when Lucky touches my hand and I realize the runner has passed by. By the time we look up, he is just a small dark figure disappearing around a corner of the school. The sound of his footsteps gradually fades away, and the empty night sky is the only witness left.

No lights are on, but the living room is drenched in moonlight.

Just as I quietly squish closed the front door, I see Dad coming in from the dining room. Why does this have to be the one time he notices me?

"Don't turn the light on. It'll hurt my eyes."

"Where have you been, Kate?"

"You want to talk to me now?"

"I am so sorry about the other night. Talk to me about anything, anytime."

He pulls me by the elbow to sit down next to him on the sofa. I wouldn't in a million years tell him about all the stuff that's happened to me today. I try to remember what Lucky said about Dad being cool and all, but then I think about what I just found out about Lucky himself. I can't believe just a year ago I thought everything was so simple.

"Dad, what does it mean when somebody has sex with somebody?"

"Oh, Kate, if you ..."

"Just tell me."

"Honestly, Kate, it can mean a lot of different things."

I hit him and hit him, and he pulls me close into his arms and holds me tight until I stop crying.

"You didn't answer my question."

"I can tell you what it meant to me. Once I made love to your mother, I never needed to even look at another woman again. Men look at women, lust after them. I'm sure you know that, but I didn't have to. She made me happy, in every way. After all that's happened in the last few years, I'm not so sure it's normal. Maybe it was dull to her, me being that way. But that's how it was for me. That's how it is for me."

"Mom was so lucky."

"Well, Kate, she didn't think so, in the end."

"Dad, I didn't realize how much it hurt you – Mom leaving, I mean. I mean I just didn't think about it."

We're in the kitchen because he insists on making me dinner.

He doesn't notice that I'm moving all around, trying to keep my bloody sock out of his sight.

"You lost your mother."

"Mom's not living here, but she'll always be my Mom. She'll still want me to be her daughter. But she never wants to see you again. That must hurt a lot worse."

He doesn't answer, just keeps chopping on an omelet he's making.

"Kate, I have to tell you what's happening in our divorce. You mother is saying she wants to have custody of you."

"Well, I'm not going with her."

"She's going to ask you to take her side, to help her get custody."

"I just won't do it."

"Then I promise you I'll fight for you."

"Why is this even coming up? She's the one who left. She never asked me to go with her and I never said I would."

"I need to tell you something. Something I didn't tell you before because I was trying to protect her."

There are lots of secrets in this little family, I'm finding out.

"What?"

Just get it over with. Tell me what else she did to me.

"She didn't even ask for custody. From the first, the idea was that I was to have custody of you."

"Good."

"But she's changed her mind. Now she's asking for custody of you – I think to scare me."

"Scare you?"

"Scare me into turning over Alexander's Woods to her and Anton. The important point is, I don't think she really even wants to take you with her. She's just using you, sort of like a pawn in her game. Anyway, that's how it seems to me."

"I'm not surprised at anything she would do."

Lucky and I are in the basement together.

"Don't worry. He's asleep. He didn't hear me. It took forever creeping down the steps. Your mother called twice around dinner time."

"Okay."

"Okay? How can you say that? Your mother will call the cops if you don't show up there soon."

"I've been thinking." Lucky looks around at the basement, which is a horror of old junk and mechanical contraptions, lit only by the tiniest glow from a casement window. "Is there any way you can get some kind of soft thing down here I can sleep on?"

"Sleep on? Your mother's going to be calling the cops soon."

"I got to stay here until my urine will test negative. Look, if you can get me your Dad's cell phone, I'll call Diane. She'll call my mother. I figured out something she can say."

"Lucky, I found out my mother is asking for custody of me, but she'll trade me for Alexander's Woods."

"Anton!"

"Yeah, and Freeland. All of them. Nothing is like it seems. The whole world's morphing."

"Including me, right? I'm not who you thought I was."

Is he?

"I guess not."

"It was only a dream, that I could be on a level with you, Kate. But it was a good dream while it lasted. And you're helping me anyway. I'll never forget this."

"Lucky, if you get put away for years like Freeland said, and we don't ever see each other again, I want you to remember one thing, forever. This one was my fault."

"Kate. Stop worrying. I'll see you tomorrow morning at Spit Musical Chairs."

Chapter 18

"There was a terrible crime committed last night. I'm really sorry to have to tell you that one of your fellow students, Randy Johnson, was shot and killed. It did not happen on school property. He was found in Alexander's Woods, about a half-mile down the trail."

From the moment I heard those footsteps racing up the trail, I knew it was a murder. And I'm not really surprised it's Johnson. I know I'm supposed to come forward and tell the police, or Mr. Freeland, or somebody, what I saw.

"This is a sad occasion. But I have to tell you some important information right away. There is no need to panic. This did not happen on school grounds. The police are already questioning a suspect right now. The suspect is not a student.

"But the police have let me know that this is not the first time there have been reports of gunfire in Alexander's Woods. For this reason, I am advising all students, at the request of the police, to stay out of the woods at all times. Those woods are not connected with the educational experience offered in this school in any way.

"All students will be given letters explaining this today, and I want each of you to make sure your parents see this tonight. We're also mailing a copy to each parent."

When Principal Freeland finishes, he stands off to the side. Somebody gets up to the microphone and says that counselors will come around to each class over the next week to help us deal with our feelings. Johnson's guard gets up and picks up her coat and trudges away. Nobody told her before now that Johnson was dead.

Lucky appears beside me, hunched low in the chair.

"I'm staying out of sight of Freeland. If he sees me, he's going to get me busted."

"Lucky, did you know it was him? Did you know it was Johnson?"

"I figured. You told me he was out there."

"Who would do that to him?"

"I can think of a lot of people."

"I'm sure after a while I will feel really sorry, but ..."

"I know."

"Lucky, how did you stay away all night without you mother calling the cops? What did you and Diane say to your mother?"

"Oh, easy. Christian youth group. Emergency rescue technician ride-along. The whole night shift. Watched someone patch up a bleeding ankle."

Chapter 19

The Grief Counselor, Mr. Henry, has a long ponytail going grey, and square, wire-rimmed glasses. He won't sit at the teacher's desk. He pulls one of the kid's desks around backwards and faces us from our level. He tries to make us push all of our desks around so that we're in a big circle, but there's not really enough room for a circle, so we end up with just a big jumble of desks. People are quiet. They know we are going to talk about death.

"Everybody comfortable?" He looks over us like a hen sitting on her eggs. Then he answers his own question by nodding his head. He slides closer to the kids.

"Okay, okay. Good." He looks right at any kid who will look back at him. He smiles at us, one at a time, like he's catching this vibe of love coming off of us or something.

"I know how hard it is to lose a classmate. It's like losing a member of your family. I know how hard it is to go on, knowing that the person you talked with and worked with and played with is not here and will never be here again.

"The first thing you need to know, and I'm telling you this as someone who has a lot of experience in these things, is that some of you may need to cry, and if you need to cry, you needn't be ashamed of that. There's nothing wrong with having these feelings of grief, nothing wrong with letting those feelings of grief out and showing them to others."

As far as I can tell, the class is more laid back than it's ever been since the first day Johnson was dragged in here by his guard.

"Let's talk to each other now." Mr. Henry's voice is loud now, and he turns his head slowly to try to catch each person's eye. "It's good to be able to express our grief. Remember, if you have certain feelings, there is probably at least one other person who feels the same way. There might be many who feel that way. And we want to hear your feelings. And we want to validate them."

Lucky and I are whispering.

"Lucky! Shouldn't I just tell them? It was Rat who did it, don't you think?"

Mr. Henry is looking at me, asking my name.

"Kate. Kate," he repeats, "what emotions are you feeling right now?"

"I don't want to say."

"Why not?"

"It's not right."

"Not right that Randy Johnson should have to die?" Mr. Henry's voice is soft.

"I guess so."

"If that's not what you meant, it's okay to say what you do mean. If we're not honest about how we feel, we're presenting a false front, and that makes it hard for people to reach us, and it keeps people isolated from each other."

"Okay. I know I should feel bad because somebody died, and I do in a way, but mostly I feel relieved that I can come to this class now and Johnson won't be here any more."

Mr. Henry is quiet for a long time, working his jaw.

"It's very normal to feel resentment," his voice has dropped down to a whisper. "Even against the deceased. But that's usually just a mask we subconsciously put on to hide our real feelings of loss."

"You said I should tell how I feel."

"He almost raped her," Diane shouts out.

"Sometimes," Mr. Henry's voice gets louder, "in the face of a traumatic event, like a death, we feel anger against the deceased for deserting us. That anger gets expressed in different ways in different people. It's not uncommon for someone's first reaction to be an accusation against the deceased."

"No, it really happened," Lucky says. "He tried to rape her. What I want to know is, why did they put him in this class? Johnson was out of control. Anybody could see that."

"Why did they pretend he could be in this class? He wasn't learning anything."

"It's a program," Mr. Henry says, "and a philosophy. It's a nationwide program. The idea is to help ..."

"Help who?" I'm almost shouting. Mr. Henry stops, looks at me.

"Kate, believe me, I can feel your anger all the way up here. Maybe some of this anger comes from guilt, because we never accepted him, and we know we should have accepted him. He did have the right to be your classmate, to be mainstreamed, in a regular class."

"Why? Really. Who was this supposed to help?" This is Lucky.

"The law says Randy is like any other person." Mr. Henry smiles at us, but I can tell he won't answer our actual question. "Like any other boy, he was entitled ..."

"He couldn't even count to ten. Everybody laughed at him." Diane's voice is loud again. "I laughed at him myself, sometimes right to his face. Now somebody killed him."

Mr. Henry forgets about everybody but Diane. He smiles at her like he's her dear father. He doesn't talk any more about why Johnson was in our class. His eyes are now round and soft. His voice is crooning. He's finally found his groove.

"And how does that make you feel?" he says.

The driveway and all the sidewalks around the school are clogged with freaked-out parents double-parked and milling all around. One mother is standing frozen in the middle of the concrete walk, facing us, her poppy eyes fixed wide open and her face screwed up like a cartoon. She stares at Lucky's shaved head. He gets in her face and whispers "Boo!" and she yelps and runs away.

"Don't you think it was Rat?"

Diane, Lucky and I are looking for a place to go that isn't so crowded with cars and vans and parents.

"He might hurt somebody a little bit for a joke, but I can't see him killing a kid on purpose."

"Rat told me he was going to shoot Mr. Folsom for being gay," Diane says.

A couple of parents near us on the sidewalk suddenly go quiet. Lucky motions for us to move away. We get together again on the grass on the school's front lawn.

"I never heard that before."

"He said it that day you and I got drunk in the woods. I think you were passed out by then. I just figured it was bullshit."

"How do you know Mr. Folsom is gay?"

"Oh come on, Kate. Thirty-Five. Unmarried. So jittery. All that self-torture. Everyone knows."

People start listening to us again. Diane pulls out her cell phone.

Carl pulls up a few minutes later. We still don't talk about what's happened because Carl goes on and on about a case of cold beer he has in the trunk and how he has to be at work at six-thirty. He says he has to stop drinking at two beers to stay under the DUI limit. Lucky says his father told him it was five.

Diane has a deck on the back of her house, with big shade umbrellas still out from the summer and set up for privacy from the sides. We hang outside on deck chairs and recliners, peeping into all the back yards of her neighborhood, soaking up the sun.

Carl and Diane lie back in matching recliners and hold hands.

"You two remind me of my Mom and Dad when I was little, sitting out in the back yard staring at the garden."

"Ain't it great?" Carl says.

"Diane and I used to make fun of them. We called it 'slow motion recreation.'"

"But it's our spot now," Diane says. "It's our own. It's different. It's fun."

"You have to take your fun where you can get it." Carl is trying to join the conversation. "Life is tough enough as it is."

Carl doesn't notice that Diane makes a face at this remark. I don't see how Diane could possibly know if his life is hard. He works six days a week and she has never worked a day. She's making a face because he just said what her parents always say – life is hard. Carl is like her parents in a lot of ways, but she doesn't see it. She's even starting to bicker with him about how he spends his money.

Diane's twelve-year-old sister, Lisa, opens the back door and walks onto the deck in a sweatshirt and shorts.

"Oh shit! I forgot she was here today."

Lisa is cool for a kid, and I know Diane likes her. Diane's so much edgier now that she's with Carl. Lucky's never even seen Lisa before, but he calls her out like we're all best friends. I say hi to her real nice too, but I don't mean it. She shouldn't be here right now. She walks around the deck, looks at the beer, leans against the deck rail. Her long stick legs goosebump in the cold.

"Carl, can I have a beer?"

"No," Diane snaps. "Come on, Lisa. I want to be alone with my friends right now."

"There's nobody else to hang with. And you guys aren't as bad as you make out you are, anyway."

"Isn't Adrian home? Can't you go over there for a while?"

Lisa leans back against the deck railing and looks at Carl. She figures out right then that Carl isn't going to do anything that Diane doesn't want him to do. "If I'm not getting any beer, I'll go. But you owe me one."

After she goes, we all sip in silence for a minute. I don't really like beer. I'm still dying to know if Lucky thinks Rat did it, but I don't want to talk about it in front of Carl. But Carl is the one who actually brings it up.

"Hey, did you guys hear this? Somebody at the end of shift last night told me someone was shot in Alexander's Woods."

We stare at him.

"What? Is that just a story?"

"You haven't heard?" Diane's voice is more than surprised. Worse than surprised.

"You forget, honey. I work six-thirty to two every day. When I'm off, I work on my car, or sleep, or go out with you."

"Johnson, the guy we told you about, who was attacking Kate." Diane catches my eye, softens, explains. "That's the kid who was shot. Who was killed."

"Oh my God! Who did it?"

"Carl, if they knew, I think they'd put that person in jail."

"Don't talk to me like I'm stupid, Diane. I just hadn't heard."

She leans over and puts a hand on his arm and rubs it slowly up and down.

"Sorry, honey. Sorry."

I look away. The sun paints the edges of the clouds as they slide by. Diane climbs into his chair and they really get started. When Diane squeaks out an excited little "oh!" I see Lucky squirm in his chair. I'm wondering what dirty little pictures are playing in his mind. After embarrassing both of us half to death, Carl and Diane finally decide to go inside. Then my heart really starts pounding and my throat dries up. I used to think I was in love with Lucky, but now I don't know what to think. Say something, Kate.

"When she starts criticizing Carl, she sounds just like her

mother."

"Love in the 'burbs. Ain't it grand?"

I guess you know a lot about love, I think.

"I guess you know a lot about love," I say.

He sits up so fast his chair screeches. Lucky's hair is growing out, his scalp peppered with tiny black dots like the face of a man who hasn't shaved. He's leaning forward like he's ready to leap out of the chair.

"Kate, I ..."

"I'm sorry. Forget I said that. Please? Lucky, where will you hide out tonight?"

"Tonight? Back to my mother's. The Christian Youth rescue ride-along scam is pretty much played out."

"But can't they still test you? Wouldn't you still test positive after two days?"

"The cops are not going to worry about me smoking pot when somebody was just murdered right there in the woods."

He's just two feet away, so smart, with those deep, dark eyes and that gorgeous man-boy body. It's almost like we are normal, just having a talk, as if things were not so twisted up between us. I'm aching to touch him, to have him hold me – but the idea still half-turns my stomach. Everything's swirling around like a tornado. I hold on tight to the aluminum frame of the lounge chair just to keep myself from flying off.

"God, Lucky, look at those streaks across the sky. It's so great to be here all alone, away from school, away from my father, away from the cops, away from everybody."

"You're not all alone."

"Look at those windows, like they're on fire from the sunset. There's something sad about all these houses, all so closed up and quiet, don't you think? Why doesn't anybody ever come outside? It's so beautiful, but so lonely too. Do you know what I mean?"

Lucky pulls his chair closer to mine and holds my wrists

with his fingertips, almost like he's taking my pulse. My chair is shooting through space.

"I'm sorry."

His arm is lean and muscular, angled out with bones at the elbows, covered with a fine layer of dark hair. I'm trying not to look at his face because just looking at his arm is doing it for me.

The door crashes open and Carl charges out on the deck, a plastic six-pack of beer dangling from his hand. He stomps to the railing and starts pouring beers down his throat one after another. Lucky starts moving toward him slowly, like a cop in a movie stalking some nutcase with a gun – put it down, son, and nobody gets hurt.

Diane is in the kitchen, her eyes all puffy and red. I'm looking at her, thinking the two of us are like a demonstration of what boys can do to you.

"You should see the look on *your* face, Kate."

"It's because I've never seen you cry."

She giggles and sniffs and blows her nose.

"It's not the same as it was at first. Maybe I don't really love him."

I can maybe imagine going for a ride with Carl in his car if there was nothing else to do, but that's about it. I don't know what to say.

"No one ever loved me before, not like he does. Carl's so real, it's so real, but sometimes I still feel like shit."

Diane and I both have a high opinion of our intelligence, but now I'm thinking maybe we are actually some kind of defectives, judging by our luck with our chosen boyfriends.

Carl has already drunk too much beer and is sagging in a lounge chair with his arms and legs out in all different directions.

"Man, you've got to work in an hour. You're going to lose your job, man." As he says this, Lucky snatches the rest of the six-pack and takes it inside. Diane comes out on the deck, red eyes and all, and pulls up a chair next to Carl. When Carl takes her hand, she stares at him until he drops it.

"It doesn't have to be like this," he says.

"What do you mean?"

"How am I supposed to know what you're thinking all the time? It'll take me a whole lifetime to figure you out, Diane. But we do have a whole lifetime, don't we?"

It gets really, really quiet on the deck for a really long time. Lucky finally breaks this awesome silence by asking me to go for a walk. Still, the two of us can't talk either.

The neighborhood is still pretty much empty as the light in the sky starts to fade. The houses are bigger than the ones on my street. All of them are newer, with two stories or more, decks, most with attached garages. All the lawns are neatly clipped. All the leaves are raked. The doors are tightly closed. Pretty, bright houses of grey and beige and white vinyl siding, set back just a few feet from the street on their own little squares of green. But the main thing about these houses is there's nobody in them. I get this really weird feeling, because the houses are so closed off and empty and quiet under the fading pink light of the sky, that Lucky and I have our own sort of privacy right out here on the street.

"Somebody lives in every one of these houses." I'm hugging my own arms against the chill.

"No kidding."

"I mean, the houses all look so friendly. But they're so tight. Either you're in, or you're out. And if you're out, where do you go?"

"I never thought about that."

"Don't you ever feel like, 'where am I supposed to be?'"

"Yeah. I'll make my own place some day. It won't be like

this. You'll have a place some day too, Kate. It will be better than this."

"Wherever I am, I won't ever leave my child."

We walk along for a minute.

"For now, I just pretend I have two houses."

That just makes me scream. "But you don't! Rudi is in one of those houses. And Anton is in one of mine." I grab his wrists so he can feel how much I mean this, but he jerks free and walks ahead by himself.

"Like I *said*, I just *pretend*!" Then he slows down until I catch up. "When it's your place, Kate, and your child, you can do what you want. And you would never do what your Mom did."

"I don't know if I'm good or not."

"I do."

"But look at us. Look at where we are right now."

"What do you mean?" He's truly puzzled. "We're fine."

And that is something amazing about him, and I see it over and over. If you don't keep reminding him of what's wrong, he always goes back to thinking that everything is fine.

"Okay, we're not starving, or getting our legs blown off in some war, but ... well, even if we are okay, Lucky, what are we supposed to do now?"

He stops. "Now? Now? Keep walking, I guess." We do. "Kate, I know this much. You would never leave your kid. You would never do anything so wrong."

We're out on the street, deliciously alone, and he's actually making me believe that I'm not really such a jerk. The street is empty, but I catch myself thinking it wouldn't be so bad if somebody would come out of one of those silent houses and see us together right now.

"Gotta get to work!" At least, that's what I think Carl is saying. He knows he can't drive but he's dead sure he can do his job. Diane is dying.

"Gotta work. Ain't going to be a fucking pauper like my father."

"Your father's poor?" I'm just babbling, I know.

"He works at a 7-11 in Florida. Lives in a room. Used to have a business here in Glenwood. Cheated out of everything. I'm not losing my job."

Lucky doesn't have a license but he says he can drive. We all crowd into Carl's Camaro. Carl sits up front with Lucky to show him how the controls work. Diane and I sit in the back, like when old people go out together. The car bucks and leaps forward, then jerks to a stop.

"I thought you knew how to drive."

"A backhoe."

"A *backhoe*?" Diane shrieks. "A *backhoe*? Here, let me drive. I have operated a sewing machine."

"Wait. It's gotta be ... It's gotta be basically the same."

We lurch and jerk all the way across Glenwood with Diane laughing hysterically in the back seat. Lucky gets pissed at this, and I can see him concentrating harder. Carl's passed out, but he jerks awake at every stop. At last, we pull up to a high fence outside of the printing press where Carl works. He raises his fist as he walks away.

"Leave the car at Diane's house, the keys on the right front tire."

"I have a cool idea about driving back." Diane puts a hand on Lucky's shoulder. "I wonder if we could see any better if we turned the lights on."

When we get back, Lisa is sitting on the front porch in the dark.

"Locked out, you geniuses."

The houses are just silhouettes now.

"Things will be all right, Kate."

We're walking fast, watching our shadows crisscross in the streetlights. Lucky thinks I'm a better person than I really am. I would give anything to be that person.

"Why is Carl so worried about being poor?"

"His father lost everything. My father told me about it a long time ago."

"It's awesome to me that you know everything about what's going on. I mean it. How did Carl's father lose everything?"

"His partner cheated him out of all of his money."

"Can people just do that and get away with it?"

"Do kids cheat on tests? Do lawyers tell lies? My father says a lot of businessmen will cut your throat for a buck."

The houses in the development grow darker in the fading light. We're still walking together, fast, stepping forward on the hard ground even though the hypnotizing beauty of the sky has faded.

"And, Kate. The thing is. Carl's father's partner was Anton."

Chapter 20

Principal Freeland is out in front of the school. Hysterical parents wait in long lines of cars and vans to drop their kids right at the door, as if the person who killed Johnson down on the trail at night is going to pop up and kill a normal person in front of the school at 7:30 in the morning. Then Freeland lords it over a community meeting in the auditorium with his strong jaw and his deep voice, and people do whatever he wants because they're so scared. I don't get it. If anyone would know about Johnson and the people who might want to kill him, it would be me, and I'm not the least bit scared. And no matter what the Grief Counselor says, and no matter what I did to him, I still don't feel the least bit sorry that Johnson is gone.

It doesn't even bother me when the police come to school and pick me up. I hear Lucky talking about Corporal Walton all the time, almost like they're friends.

"Didn't I see you at the Seven Eleven last Saturday night? Only you had on regular clothes and an earring in one ear."

"Must have been my evil twin brother."

Walton takes me into a little cubicle to ask me questions. I can't believe people are supposed to say stuff about things like murders here, where there's hardly any privacy. He tells me I'm not a suspect, and I have to laugh. If I was the main suspect in a murder, they wouldn't send the guy who looks like an overgrown teenage boy to interrogate me.

"Look," he says, "I know Lucky didn't do it, but why won't he tell me anything?"

"Lucky didn't do it. I was with him when we heard the shot go off."

"You didn't see it happen?"

"No. It sounded like it was kind of far away, down the trail."

"So," he sits back and smiles, "who do you think shot Randy Johnson?"

"I don't know. I saw Rat shoot this rifle off in the woods once. But I didn't see Rat that night."

"We know about the rifle. It wasn't Rat."

I look at him.

"It wasn't even a rifle." He raises an eyebrow. "It was Lucky's father's gun."

He puts his hand on top of mine, in a nice way, but it makes me catch my breath and scrambles my brains.

One of the things that they might have found when they examined Randy Johnson's body was a mark on his face where I hit him really hard with that stick. What he was doing was so sickening, and he was doing it thinking about me. He tried to talk to me right then, but I was really scared. Corporal Walton looks at me, and I'm thinking I might have been the last person Johnson ever talked to alive. If that's true, then the last thing he ever said was that he loved me.

"It's important that we solve this case before somebody else gets hurt. Can you understand that? It doesn't seem like Lucky does. Any information can be helpful."

The whole thing is a little scarier if it isn't Rat. I tell him about seeing Johnson on the bridge a couple hours before he was shot.

"Did he try to attack you then?"

"No. I don't think so. He did try to reach his hand out to me."

"And you hit him with a stick?"

"Yes."

"In the face. Did he touch you at all on the bridge?"

"No."

"He was, like, reaching for you? That's why you hit him with the stick?"

Walton is trying to make an excuse for me. It has never occurred to me before that I need an excuse to hit Johnson with a stick.

"Did he hurt you?"

"No, not really. He didn't do anything to me in the woods that day."

"Did you tell Lucky that Johnson had hurt you?"

"No."

I tell Walton most of what happened that might. I leave out the part about Rudi being with Lucky. And one other part.

Walton pulls back like he is studying me. His eyes are dark brown, and his head is shaved. His hair will grow in blonde, not dark like Lucky's.

"Who else knew where that gun was hidden, besides you and Lucky?"

"I guess his ..."

"... father." Walton's eyes search mine. "Now, can you see why Lucky won't tell us anything?"

I stare back. "Earl would never do anything like that."

"Can you tell me what kinds of things you might have seen in the woods in the couple of weeks before the shooting?"

"You mean drinking?"

"No. I'm not interested in that group that goes down there and does alcohol, pot and stuff. Any hard drugs? Any fighting, threats, weapons, people getting hurt."

"Rat pulled a knife once on Lucky, but he just ran away when Lucky didn't get scared."

"Did you ever witness any strange behavior, like sadistic

stuff, or people even talking about cutting people up, or torturing anybody, or even animals?"

"Animals?"

"Anything. Anybody."

"Did that happen?"

"I just need to know if you saw anything like that."

Chapter 21

Lucky wants to be the first to walk the trail after the police remove the crime scene tape, so he leaves his house early and walks through the woods to school, and I meet him at the top of the trail. He is walking fast, his cheeks red, his backpack bouncing up and down on his shoulder like it's weightless, his breath puffing white. The high weeds on both sides of the trail are covered with frost.

"I saw pieces of police tape on some tree near the bridge."

"I don't ever want to go down there again."

"Oh, Kate, it'll be fine. You can go into the woods again."

He always says things will be fine.

"That cop, Walton, told me that Johnson was shot with your father's gun."

"I always thought that was our gun, from the sound of it."

"You didn't tell me that before."

It kind of sucks that Lucky and I are still playing games.

"I didn't tell the cops either. I was hoping they wouldn't figure it out."

"Because ...?"

"Think about it, Kate. If it's our gun, and it's not me, who is it?"

The driver, a guy who works for Lucky's father, kicks a whole pile of trash off the seat so we can sit in the cab. Lucky's father was released this morning. The truck cuts into a narrow alley between two buildings that line the main street of Glenwood – mostly ratty old stores in the first floors of old houses. I've never seen what's behind, and it's fifty times worse, with faded brown-shingled walls, mazes of old wooden stairways, potholes full of water. Lucky's father's office is up a creaky wooden staircase. Inside, the light is dim except for one bright fluorescent desk lamp. Papers are scattered on the desk and on other tables around the office.

Earl sits with mud-caked boots propped on top of the desk, looking at some of the papers. There is an empty beer bottle on the desk. An electric heater is in the corner, its red elements facing him. His leather chair lets out a loud squeal when he sits up.

"It was our gun? Yeah, I figured. The cops held me in the station all night. I didn't tell them anything."

The only sound is the buzz of the electric heater.

"I can't believe it! You guys suspect each other!"

The heater buzzes again.

"Dad, I didn't really think you did it. I just ..."

"... didn't want to take any chances. Yeah, I'm with you, Lucky. Looks like we did nothing but make ourselves both suspects. Hey, the two of us better not try any actual crimes!"

Earl laughs.

And that is it. They are okay. I've seen girls' arguments over nothing last fifty times as long. But then Lucky starts another argument.

"Dad, you've got to get rid of Rudi."

"Son, she's ..."

"Get rid of her, Dad. If you don't, I'll never be able to be with you."

"What if Rudi don't smoke or drink in the house? She'd do that for me."

"It's too late. Mom knows I've been going there. I can't sneak over there any more. Can't you please just get rid of her?"

Earl plants his feet on the floor and runs his fingers through his hair. The empty beer bottle falls off the desk. Nobody pays attention to it rolling around on the floor.

"Son, she's nothing like your mother, I know. But you got to remember that I wasn't good enough for your mother. Rudi met me in a bar and then pulled me out of it – I think because she loves me. I don't smoke any more. I don't drink hardly anything like I used to. And it's all because I found somebody way down low like me, and maybe we want to make each other just a little better. She's all I have."

Mr. Folsom is pacing back and forth in front of the class, mumbling to himself. There aren't any equations on the board. He hardly notices Lucky and I slip in late and sit in the back.

"First, everybody blamed the school for what happened to Randy Johnson. Now they're blaming me. It isn't as if I didn't try to help the boy. It isn't as if I didn't try to get his aide in here every day. Now they're investigating me for 'negligent supervision.' What does that mean when you're supposed to be teaching a boy that age and size who doesn't have the social skills of a two-year-old?"

"It's been like this since the start of class," Diane whispers.

"And why I am the only teacher investigated? I'd love to have the answer to that, I really would. The school board attorney called a meeting last night of all Randy Johnson's teachers. We are not allowed to talk to students about Randy Johnson's death, or how he did in school here, or if he was dangerous, or why he was here in the first place. So I guess if you students are going to learn anything from this tragedy, you're going to have to figure it out on your own."

Freeland comes in quietly and pulls Lucky and me out of the classroom.

"Lucky, you're going to be arrested."

He takes us outside where a police car is waiting. A cop gets out of the car and opens the back door for Lucky. I know it's my fault, because I didn't get my father to go along with Freeland's plan like I promised. Why are the police so worried about Lucky smoking pot when there's a killer in the woods? It's still my fault, though. It's like Lucky is the guy with the hood over his face who will be beaten for anything wrong the rest of us do. Neither one of the cops in the car will answer me or even look up.

"Wait right here," Freeland says to the cops, then points for me to follow him back inside.

"I guess my message to you wasn't clear enough last time."

"He's not going to be locked up just for smoking pot."

"Your friend's fingerprints were found on the gun that killed Johnson. Even if he didn't shoot Johnson – which I think he did – it's a felony to carry a gun while on probation. Do you know what will happen if he's found guilty of just a handgun violation? It's a five-year mandatory sentence. No parole. No sissy juvenile court. Your friend is in handcuffs in the police car right outside. They're just waiting to talk to me. Once they charge him, it's mandatory. Doesn't matter if the judge feels sorry for him. Five years. Real jail. The older convicts do what they want with him. Use him like a piece of meat."

I've already had nightmares about Lucky being locked up in jail and beaten for years, while everyone outside goes on with their ordinary lives. Lucky told me the dumbest thing I can do is show that I'm afraid, so I hold everything in, clench my hands at my sides and keep my feet flat on the floor so my legs won't shake. This is the best I can do. Freeland has beaten me down. There has to be a point where even Lucky will break and turn scared or turn mean, and then he'll never be the same again. And I know they will never let me see him again until they've broken him like that.

"What do you want?"

"I already told you exactly what I want. I want your father to give Alexander's Woods to your mother. I want it to happen within 48 hours. *No more fucking around.*"

Why is he doing this to me? Then I hear a huge clang from some kind of construction machine outside. It kind of wakes me up, and then I'm thinking bigger, trying to put things together – thinking like Lucky. When you put all the things together it makes sense. You have to be blind not to notice it, but I didn't notice before that the school is right next to Alexander's Woods, that Freeland was promising somebody he'd have the school torn down, that Anton wants the woods torn down for his development, and that Freeland wants Dad to give the woods to Anton.

"I want you to know, Kate, that I will do *anything* to make that transaction happen."

My mother coming to the school. My mother calling Freeland all the time. I should have known it wasn't about me. I should have known it had nothing to do with me. But I don't care any more if my mother is concerned about me or not. I don't even care if she and her lover Anton do tear down the woods. I care about Lucky.

"I told the police to wait just ten minutes," Freeland adds in his slithery voice, "before they take him away. They're ready to take him. Are you going to say yes now, or should I let them take him? As soon as they get to the station, they can start drawing up the handgun charges. Then no one can stop it." He starts to get up from his chair.

"I'll do whatever you want. I'll do whatever you want." What am I worth, anyway? I did this to Lucky. I'm the one who should be treated like dirt. "Do you want me to get down on my knees and beg? Because I will."

I walk out obediently to the police car behind Freeland. He puts his hand on my shoulder and steers me like his little pet. Lucky sees us from inside the car and gives me just the saddest look. Freeland talks a while with the two cops, but they still don't let Lucky out of the car. They take him away anyway.

"What!"

"It's just for one night in the police lockup. So you won't forget this time."

I pull his hand off and run down the school driveway after the car.

All the way home I'm telling myself that it won't hurt Dad that much to give up the woods. It's just land, after all. He wants to keep it because his mother gave it to him. Now I'll be telling him to give it up. Grandma will be rolling over in her grave. He loves that land, but he is sick, I know. He thinks he doesn't have anything else but that land, but he's so wrong.

I'm only now starting to feel how much Dad must hurt. It must hurt so much to know the one you love is going to go on living, but you will never be a part of their life. It must be worse than if they die. If Lucky is sent away, they won't ever let me see him again. They will put him in a cage and just slowly turn him into some kind of convict animal. Every day I will feel it happening, and every day I will know it is my fault that it is happening.

Dad told me that morning that the rumor going around the county was that Freeland was going to be made Superintendent of Schools. Maybe that will be his payment for scamming up this land for Anton.

I'm so mad thinking about all this that I'm not looking where I'm going. On a corner lot I see a yard decoration, a big corny plastic statue of a deer. Then I get real close and look again. Then it turns its head and looks right back at me.

It's a real deer, a buck with huge brown eyes and giant antlers. We are ten feet apart, and we both freeze. I see more and more deer lately, pushed out of the woods, eating people's grass and flowers and stuff. Once I saw one lying dead in the street and I turned away and cried. But this guy doesn't seem like any kind of sad victim. He looks like he thinks he belongs there. I think he knows I'm going to sell out to the developers the last piece of woods in Glenwood.

I love his sleek body and his thick tan coat, but my eyes are drawn back to his eyes. It's true: I'm going to betray you too. I can't keep looking at those eyes. I turn my head and just walk right past him, really slow, and I don't look back. He can gore me in the back right now if he wants to. He can kill me. I wonder if he knows he can save the woods right now by killing me. I don't really care if he does kill me. I almost hope that nature has that much power to save itself.

"You should have seen what happened after you left." Diane is calling on her cell phone.

"Where are you?"

"I'm in a stall in the girls' bathroom, pretending to have my period."

"What happened?"

"You won't believe this. Everybody got real quiet after they took you and Lucky out of the class. Everybody was really mad. Nobody would answer any questions about algebra. Mr. Folsom tried to talk to us, just regular, but nobody would say anything back. I felt sorry for him, but – you know, I was pissed too.

"Then he just lost it! He started screaming, 'Hey, you hate me too. Good. Let's make it a clean sweep.' He takes his hand and sweeps everything off his desk, really hard. It hits the floor and the wall and everything. Then he stands there and starts crying."

I hear some kind of commotion in the background, then Diane's voice. "No way! This stall's occupied! Go smoke somewhere else."

"Are you still there? What did everybody do?"

"Nothing. Nothing. He looked so sad. You know his hair, it's never looked very good, but when he started crying his face fell apart and he looked all craggy and old with his greasy, stringy hair hanging all down. Then he got real quiet, like he was ready to go postal or something, but then he just said the saddest thing of all.

"'This school,' he says, 'isn't really going to help you. It's all way, way too screwed up. If any of you really want to get to the moon, you're going to have to make it on your own.'"

"God. I used to think about what he said, the moon, all the time."

"I know."

"Come over to my house."

"I can't. They finally figured out something weird happened and they have people in the halls looking for all the kids who split."

I ask her if she thinks Freeland will keep his word if I get my father to give up the woods, but her phone goes dead right while we're talking. Then I just stand and look out the living room window at the leaves slowly smothering the lawn. I realize that I didn't have to ask her about Freeland. I already know the answer myself.

The phone rings again and I pick it up fast.

"Hey, what's up now?"

"Kate." It's Freeland's low, creepy voice. I get ready to hear some lies.

"I want you to be comfortable," he says, "that we have a deal."

"What does that mean?"

"Why did you run away?"

"They took Lucky."

"You think you'll never see him again?"

"I know what I saw."

"Stay where you are. Stay where you are now, and keep your word."

"You're going to have somebody come and arrest me too?"

"Just wait there." He hangs up.

I'm sure there is some reason they could arrest me too. All of us had something to do with Johnson being dead, including me.

I just hope they arrest whoever put him in Mr. Folsom's math class in the first place.

The phone rings again. It's Dad.

"The school called me and said you ran out."

"They called you?"

"Yeah. They couldn't find your mother. I guess they had to call me. What happened?"

"They arrested Lucky. They found his fingerprints on a gun."

"Honey, you know Lucky didn't shoot that boy!"

"But they'll find a way to punish him anyway."

"I'm sure the fingerprint thing can be explained. What about you? What are you doing there? Do I need to come home?"

"No. I'm okay."

After Dad hangs up, I get the jitters so bad that I have to get out of the house, but just then the police pull up right in front. I'm not afraid of Corporal Walton, but I don't know what any of the rest of them would do to me if they had me helpless somewhere where nobody else could see. I guess I'm going to find out.

But when the car door opens, only Lucky gets out. He runs up the walk to me, and I start running and crash into him. I squeeze him in my arms and bury my face in his neck. I can feel him all the way through his jacket and sweatshirt. He's holding me tight, not sobbing like me. The familiar smell of his warm breath soaks into me, calms me down. We're stuck there in the middle of the walk because I'm holding on so tight and won't let go.

"Kate," he says, "it's okay. The cops are really pissed, but not at me, I think. I can't figure out what's going on. But they let me go." His dark eyes sparkle with curiosity.

"Come inside."

"They found my fingerprints on the gun."

We sit down on the sofa. If you gave us coffee cups and

saucers, we would look almost like old people chatting.

"Lucky, the night Johnson was killed, and we were hiding in the weeds near the school, and that guy came running out of the woods – you told me not to look up. Did you look up? Did you see who it was?"

"I don't want to talk about that night."

"Freeland told me they could put you away just for touching that gun."

"Yeah, that's what they said at the station. They didn't write anything down, though, no charges or statements or anything. Right after that they put me in a car and took me here."

"Freeland said they could put you away in adult jail for five years, with no parole. He said you'd be a twenty-year-old convict by the time you got out."

Lucky's face drops, and the damp grey day seeps inside the house. If they take him away from me, I will never be able to love anybody else. Not as much as I love him. I know they say that people love when they're old, too. But it won't be the same. We'll be old, and we'll be thinking about money and houses and jobs. We'll be bargaining, balancing one thing against another. None of it will be anything like what Lucky and I are feeling for each other right now. Who we love will never mean as much.

Chapter 22

Triandos was wonderful to me. He didn't once mention again the big promotion that the County Executive dangled in front of him and that he refused, because he knew how much my heart was wrapped up in keeping Alexander's Woods. I worked through day after day, focused on work, meetings – the harder the work, the more intense the controversy, the better it was for me. And I also had to think about Kate, where she would be each afternoon, what our plans were for dinner. The loss of Clare infected me and made bittersweet even my life with Kate. Sometimes a memory of Clare would push a tide of despair down into my chest, and the only way I could get rid of it was to suck in air suddenly and huff it off. Triandos saw me do this once.

"Are you all right?'

"Sure."

He measured me. In another second his expression softened, and his large dark eyes and bushy eyebrows grew thoughtful. He jangled the change in his pocket.

"Breathing," he said. "Good thing to do. Keep that breathing going."

Ever since Triandos gave up that promotion, I'd watched him closely, waiting to see when he would start to resent me. He had never asked me anything more about the woods. But I had watched his eyes as he turned away from me at the end of each conversation, listened for any connotation of dissatisfaction in any of the words he used, listened to see if his little jokes had a different twist now.

Nothing. Nothing at all different. The man, if anything, was more cheerful than before.

"Why?" I finally said. "I'm the stumbling block for your promotion. Why don't you resent me?"

"The stumbling block for my promotion," he said quietly, "is that I'm not a suck-up."

"But you should get promoted. You're the one who keeps this whole place going."

"That's why I've gotten as far as I have. People like the County Exec need people like me to tell them the truth about what's going on, but they also need suck-ups and people to do their dirty work."

"You really think you can only go so high without being a suck-up or a fixer?"

"Of course, Sam. And how high you can go depends on the agency you're in. You can tell how good a government agency is by how high they let the truth-tellers get. This County Exec, and his government – they're about average."

"What I really want to know is – how much do you blame me?"

"Forget it. You just want to hold onto the woods. People need to hold onto things sometimes, I guess. I've never really had a, you know, heartbreak." He looked away, out the window. "I can't imagine ..."

"Well, it's not so bad. One little obsession. I'll get over it."

"There's more to life."

"There's more to life. Things will get better. One day you'll see me walking in here with a smile on my face and a big fat check from Anton's development company in my hand. Then you'll know that I'm totally sane. It could happen."

"And when that happens, it'll be payback time." Triandos pushed back from his desk, his great eyebrows comically raised.

"I can't wait. Something's going to happen then that's never happened before. You're going to buy me lunch!"

There were some bad moments, too. Once, waking up from a daydream about Clare, I couldn't just blow it off. I rushed out of the office, crashed down the stairs, ran as far as I could until my lungs burned. The stares of the people on the sidewalks finally herded me back into my civilized role again. Things will get better. Think about Kate. Breathe. Repeat.

I was also having a real problem with cars. Whenever I'd see a woman driving a deep blue Acura like hers, the adrenaline would start and set my heart racing.

> *That deep blue car that you still drive*
> *Is just enough to keep me half alive.*
> *It rips my eyes from the road; it chokes my chest.*
> *It drives it home that I have failed the test.*

Just a normal, understandable thing for somebody who's suffered a loss? Okay, it got bad, and I followed a few of those cars. Okay, it got really bad, and my heart jumped for some blue ones that I knew were not even hers.

So what I did was stop looking at cars at all. I wouldn't let myself think about what kind or color they were. So I turned them into nothing but *traffic units*, and I'd pass them and they'd pass me, and it was all very abstract like the electric traffic map on the wall in the main lobby of the county office building.

"Dad, what are you staring at?" Kate's voice came through the screen door. I was standing under the carport after I arrived back home that afternoon, staring out at the leaf-strewn lawn, watching the red and yellow survivors clinging to the trees under the murky grey-blue sky. I was focusing on the colors. I did that sometimes after driving home, to allow myself to remember what colors were like. By the time I turned toward her voice at the screen door, Kate was already gone.

The only thing I remembered about my grandfather was the way he moved like an old man, stopping, sighing, letting out a small groan before each step. My recent troubles had taught me to think about him in a different way. I wasn't a kid any more, and I didn't need to roll my eyes at his old-man ways any more just to prove to myself that I wasn't like him. And the truth was, I was like him. I also had to stop and rest and suppress a groan. What difference did it make whether it was caused by an old man's brittle bones or a middle-aged man's broken heart?

"Lucky was here, but he's gone now." Kate rolled herself up from her position lying on the sofa. Then, suddenly, "I love you, Dad."

But her eyes seemed vacant. She sighed with a deep sadness. I'd never seen such a dispirited, defeated look on her face before.

"The police picked up Lucky again," she said then. "His fingerprints are on the gun that killed Johnson. I know he didn't do it, Dad, because I was with him when that shot went off. But they can put him away anyway. He's not supposed to even touch a gun. Freeland will make sure they put him away for years, unless we help Freeland get what he wants."

"What Freeland wants? I don't get it, Kate."

"He's in it with Anton. He wants the woods to go to Anton."

"Kate, I don't think ..."

"It's true, Dad. Lucky proved it, he proved the phony asbestos part of it. That's the real reason Lucky's going to jail. It's got nothing to do with his fingerprints on that stupid gun."

Kate seemed to bring up the woods in almost every conversation we had. When she was four years old I used to carry her on my shoulders to the edge of the woods and into the trees. She would laugh and grab the leaves and kick out until she almost fell off. She had forgotten all about those walks, but the first place she ran to when she was hit with all this sadness was the woods. Then she fell in love with a boy she met there. Stalking through those same woods as a boy, I used to feel a promise of a deep-rooted natural life waiting there for me. I must not have been bold enough to live out that promise, and it was too late now. I had let the promise of those woods die, and it seemed to be the judgment of the universe that the woods would therefore be taken away from me.

"Kate, I don't think anybody can put Lucky in jail just to get a real estate deal to go through."

"They can, Dad. They will. You think people can't be evil, Dad. You're such a sucker."

"I just don't think Freeland really can have Lucky put away."

"Dad, he smoked pot while he was on probation. And he wasn't supposed to even touch that gun because he was already on probation. They have a lot of phony reasons they can use to put him away."

There was still a little nagging rational question: how could Freeland, even if he was in on the deal with Anton and Clare, really engineer Lucky's fate to that degree? But maybe this was the kind of question that only a sucker would ask. Triandos basically called me a sucker too. Don't be such a nice guy, he said. Don't underestimate these people.

"I just have to think," I said weakly – lamely, Kate would say – "that eventually there's some kind of justice ... that it's not all in the hands of these ..."

Tears welled up in her eyes. I moved next to her on the sofa, but she stood up and crossed the room to a chair. She wiped her tears on her sleeve. She stopped crying and looked down at her hands folded in her lap.

"Dad, the only reason they let him out, even just for today, is because I promised Freeland you would turn the woods over to Anton."

"I don't want to even think about those woods." This came

out so loud it startled both of us.

"It's the only thing, Dad." Her voice was fast and panicky. "It's the only thing that can save him."

She stared at me.

"You keep bringing up the woods," I said. "I wish you wouldn't even talk about them. Those are my woods. You've been my one faithful friend through all of this. If you're on Anton's side now ... this is worse than I ever thought things could get."

She cried out and jumped up and ran out the door before I could think, her light blue jersey flashing between the trees and disappearing before I could act.

It seemed like the wound of Alexander's Woods would always be reopened. So why not just go in deeper and cut out the infection once and for all? Just give up hope, give the woods to Anton and Clare, and start life all over again? Follow the little droppings of logic.

I found myself in the car on my way to Lucky's father's place. I was familiar with the little valley under the power lines from my days as a kid roaming these woods. What was now a crushed stone road used to be a dirt path. There were no houses then – just the power lines buzzing overhead, the brush higher than my waist, the giant blue sky undoubtedly the sign of a higher power. My headlights now swept across a low log house. There were plants hanging down from the front porch ceiling and arranged on the porch floor, but they weren't any steps up to the porch. I turned my van into the driveway.

I saw Lucky right away at the back of the house, beckoning me to come up to the back deck. A big man with reddish hair and sideburns, both fringed with grey, popped out of the screen door onto the deck under the bright floodlights. He waved for me to come in, and I stumbled forward through a cacophony of barking dogs, big ones and little puppies. At one point I backed away from the drooling horde until I hit my head on a gong that was hanging from a trellis overhead.

"Hey, you set off our alarm system!" He laughed at his own joke, then waded through the wriggling dogs to shake my hand. His smile sent creases out from the corners of his eyes. I had intended to be stand-offish, telling myself that there was a chance that this guy was a murderer, but it was hard to believe that this open-faced man was anything more than the rough-edged softie that Kate made him out to be.

"I'm Earl, Lucky's father. You're Kate's father, right?"

"Yes."

"Nice kid. Real nice kid. You got to come in, have a beer or something."

"I know Lucky. Nice kid too. I can see he gets his friendly ways from you."

"Ha! You're the first one ever said there was anything good in him didn't come directly from his mother."

Lucky pulled on his father's arm as soon as we were inside in the kitchen.

"The police picked me up again, Dad. They found my fingerprints on the gun."

"So what? They know you didn't do it."

"They say it's a handgun violation anyway, just picking up the gun. Since I was already on probation. Five years' mandatory sentence."

"That's gotta be bullshit. We'll get you a lawyer if we have to. Stay here, Lucky, until the cops pick you up. Where's your mother, the big lawyer, when we really need her? I think she's way the hell out in California today."

"Corporal Walton told me. All the cops are saying Freeland is on their case to have me put away."

"Stay here with me until whenever they come."

"You and Rudi?"

"Yeah. Listen, she threw out all her stash a couple days ago. I made her swear she wouldn't bring it in again."

"I know you won't ever get rid of her."

Earl stepped to the refrigerator and pulled out a bottle of beer, opened it and took a big gulp without saying anything. He didn't offer me one.

"I need her, Lucky. I need you both."

I pushed through a swinging wooden door into a room as wide as the house, with a low, decorated windowsill at either side. The door to the kitchen swung shut behind me. There was a television with an artificial palm tree on top that looked like it was made out of pink and green pipe cleaners. The television had been left on. As I looked around for a phone, I was startled by a movement in one of the chairs. I looked and saw a thick mane of auburn hair under the glow of a table lamp. A girl or woman jumped up and stared at me, hands on hips. She was wearing tight jeans and a soft pink halter top, with a thin gold chain and crucifix dangling down into her chest. She brushed her hair back over her shoulder with one hand and stared at me like she was going to hit me with a karate chop.

"I'm Lucky's girlfriend father," I said, lamely. "I didn't think I was interrupting anybody."

"Oh." Her hands dropped and her shoulders relaxed. "You woke me up. You scared me. You're Kate's Dad."

Reaching down, she stood on one foot at a time and slipped on her shoes without breaking eye contact. It was fun to watch.

"Earl said I could use the phone."

"Oh. I'll get it for you. It's in the bedroom." Her shoes were gold, with low heels. Her stomach was tanned. A belly button ring glittered around her midsection as she turned. She handed me a portable phone, then reached and twisted that thick reddish-brown hair and let it hang in front, almost to her waist. When she brought her head up again, I saw a fine spray of freckles across her cheekbones.

"Do you need me to find a number for you?" She was businesslike, but a thin cloud of perfume, hair spray and cigarette smoke enveloped me.

"What? Oh. You know, we've never met."

She bounced down into an overstuffed chair facing the same way as mine, toward the television. All of the chairs faced the television. "I'm Rudi. The wicked stepmother."

"Oh. Yeah. I've heard about you from Kate." This didn't come out the way I intended.

"I didn't meet Earl until way after he and his wife split up."

She pulled herself to the edge of the chair and sat very straight.

"I think Kate told me that."

"Is Kate okay?"

I didn't know how to answer that one. "She's fourteen," I said. "Her parents are splitting up. Now she just ran off because she's mad at me. I hope she's at her friend Diane's by now. I do have that number somewhere."

She went back to the sofa and started watching television again as I started punching in Diane's phone number. She sat ramrod straight, with her legs crossed under her.

This time, they answered the phone at Diane's house.

"Kate, I'm over at Lucky's. I'm with him."

"Diane says they can't do that to him, just for touching that gun."

"I can't say for sure if they can, Kate. It seems a little extreme."

"They are all ... There are all such liars and cheats, Dad. They don't care about the school. They don't care about us. And the police are so dumb. They're arresting all the wrong people."

"Not everybody is a liar and a cheat. You're not."

"And they ... They knew I was so pitiful ... they could let Johnson do anything to me, and I couldn't stop them. I'm just nothing to them, Dad. They could just let Johnson ... he was so pitiful too ... they could just let him go on until he died."

"Kate, who is *they*?"

"You know. Everybody."

"Kate. I made a mistake about Johnson. I should have called the police the first time."

"It's all over now. He's all over anyway. Why don't they just leave us alone?"

"Kate, it's not all about just you and Lucky."

"Then why don't they leave us alone?"

Just as I hung up, Rudi came out of the bedroom, now wearing a white cotton blouse buttoned over her halter top. The conversation between Lucky and his father behind me in the kitchen was very quiet. Rudi went out there and brought me a beer and poured it into a chilled glass while I was finishing with Kate.

"How did you know I was thirsty?"

"I'm a barmaid."

"Do you live here?"

In college, a girl as hot as her would intimidate me so much I'd get drunk until I would start pawing at her and get my face slapped. If there was nothing to drink and I was within perfume range, I would cravenly turn my eyes away as the involuntary pulse she started raced down inside me. These methods didn't give me much experience dealing with hot chicks. But Rudi treated me like I was a trusted uncle or something. And there was something relaxing about that laid-back room, with the television on low in the distance and the slow, meandering breeze and the big windows with their cluttered, over-decorated sills.

"Yeah, I live here with Earl. I'm the one who does all the potted plants and crafts and gee-gaws." There were statues and pictures and macramé hangings and posters with corny sayings on the walls. "Earl says he hates this crap, but he laughs every time I put up another one."

"It's got ... real charm," I said.

She laughed. "It just makes me feel like this is home. My mother always had her own house back in the mountains all cluttered up. I swore I wouldn't be like her – but, first time I meet a man I really like," she shrugged, "here I go."

I found my way through the gloom to Diane's house, the tires hissing on the damp streets. Kate and Diane hadn't bothered to leave a front light on. Of course, I'd been to Diane's old house many times, years before. We used to drive Diane to gymnastic lessons with Kate. But her parents both had real careers. They moved to this upscale neighborhood and we hardly ever saw them again. Gymnastics was one good memory that Kate and I shared. Some of the trees in these new front yards had begun to grow, but they gave only a slightly softer edge to the place. These vinyl houses were all a little too big for their lots and a little too close to the street to justify their pretensions.

Kate opened the door, her face blank, and stepped aside. I felt for the light switch on the wall of the foyer and turned it on. She wouldn't look directly at me. She wore a tan jacket I'd never seen.

"Diane's?" I said, touching it.

"Yeah. Can we go?"

She stomped out of the house and down the walk toward the van, leaving me to close the house door. She jerked at the locked handle of the van door a couple of times, then let her arms go limp. When I opened it for her, she climbed in without a word.

"Kate, I can tell you've been drinking."

"We tried to make whiskey sours and get drunk. Then I started to get sick. Just sick. Nothing else."

"We'll be okay. Both of us will be okay, Kate, if we just hold on for a while longer."

"Lucky won't. He didn't kill Johnson, but he's the only one being punished."

The van hissed through the streets. Could they really do that to him?

"Dad, I don't see how I'm going to live if he's put away."

"I know you think that's going to happen ..."

"Dad, Freeland called me just now at Diane's! They're

picking up Lucky again tomorrow, this time for good."

Jesus! I thought. But I tried to hide my surprise.

"Kate, I learned today that these characters your mother is doing business with are worse than I thought. I should have been paying more attention before."

"Why don't they just leave us alone? They are all such creeps."

The asphalt road, glazed slick in the rain, slid by under the headlights. How did I get to be thirty-six years old and still be so weak?

"Dad, I want to tell you what Lucky and I did this afternoon."

I hit the brakes as the light turned red.

"Kate, if you and Lucky made love – I'm not happy about it. It's so dangerous, in so many ways."

"Dad."

"Let me finish. He is a good and decent boy. I know that you love him. That's a good thing. Very few people ever really have that."

She shrieked and started pounding the dash with her fists. I pulled to the curb and stopped.

"I don't have *anything*, Dad." She made fists and pounded the dashboard again. "I don't have anything." Thud. "I didn't do anything." Thud. "I didn't *do* anything, Dad, and I don't know why." She dropped her head and just hung forward, letting the shoulder belt restrain her, and sobbed. Still hanging forward, facing down, she went on in a flat, dead voice.

"I wanted to tell you we didn't do anything."

"I'm so glad, Kate."

"I'm not. Now I will never have that. I will never have the only thing I ever really wanted."

Her voice whined between sobs. "I thought at least I could get drunk and forget about everything. I just got sick. I can't even get drunk. The pain is never going to go away."

I caressed the back of her hand. I had to.

"I've made a lot of mistakes," I said. "I can't make all of your problems go away, Kate. But I will try not to make them worse. Tell me if I'm making them worse."

I unbuckled my seat belt and slid over into her seat, and she held me tight and sobbed and cried into my chest. I had been so blinded by my own pain that I had not seen her pain before. We were both fleeing the fire consuming the woods. We had just been burnt in different ways.

"Kate?"

She made a noise, like a whimper.

"I'm not going to lie to you. For some of this heartache stuff, there's not any cure."

She kept her head there, breathing deeply. Her face was pressed into my chest so hard I thought she might be asleep. The engine was off, the mist landing silently on the windshield. We were just past the intersection, bathed alternately in red, green and yellow.

"Kate, if I could take this pain for you, I would."

"I know."

A spasm went through her body. I tried to hold her tighter, but then I realized she was giggling.

"That's ridiculous, Dad. I'm the one who's in love with Lucky. And you know what? I wouldn't trade that with anyone."

As we drove off, I told her about Triandos, about the County Executive putting pressure all the way down the line for me to sell the woods – all this so Anton's secret development and shopping mall plan could go forward.

"See," I said, trying to make a little joke, "even Triandos is suffering because of my sick stubbornness in refusing to give up the woods."

"You're making things worse now, Dad."

I stopped.

"I mean, maybe you are kind of sick."

I just looked straight ahead, breathing. In. Out. In. Out. Good thing to do. Keep that breathing going.

"But you're right, Dad. Those woods are yours. You can't just let Anton take them from you."

She just said the same thing that Earl said, that Triandos said.

"So how am I making things worse?"

"Don't say you're sick, Dad."

She saw the car before I did – the deep blue Acura, parked under the street light in front of our house.

"Oh, look. If it isn't Mom's car."

I stopped and flicked my high beams on it. I should have been overjoyed to see Clare's car here. It still jolted me to see it, but now my soul was wincing, because it knew I was going to be hit, again.

We took our time in the driveway so that Kate could straighten up.

"Don't let her smell your breath."

Chapter 23

Clare stood up almost formally when we came in. Was she trying to make the point that this wasn't her home any more? Kate said hi quickly and ran up the stairs to her room.

"Sit down, Clare."

Her eyes were tired. It was a languorous, reluctant look, more sexy to me even than her usual self-controlled perkiness. When we were sleeping together, this look meant she didn't want to be approached. Now, she pulled back, waiting for something. I knew what it was. I was expected to beg, if only with my eyes.

"Sam, I was hoping we could talk, and maybe reach some final kind of agreement on our – arrangement."

Divorce, she meant, but she didn't say the word. Was this just an accident, or couldn't she say the word either? Was she lost too? Was her every cell vibrating in anticipation like mine? I tried to read her eyes.

"You don't want to talk?" She raised her eyebrows.

"Um ... yeah, I guess we should." I knew we shouldn't, or at least I shouldn't. I was in no shape to bargain for myself.

I wanted to tell her how much I missed her, but I had done that one too many times. Nobody wanted to hear about that. Maybe the day would come when she and I would laugh and cry together over this whole episode of confusion and temporarily misplaced love, but it would not come from my begging for it.

"Sam, when divorced people have children, their relationship never really ends. They have to talk to each other, no matter who has custody. They have to plan together."

"Mmm."

"No matter what's happened to you and I, Sam, we really should reach agreement on Kate's custody, and all the other things."

"Do you really think we can still be friends?"

"Sam, I don't want to share my life with you any more. But I wish you well."

I knew my stare was blank.

"I think we can be friends." She knew what I wanted to hear, and she wanted the deal to go through, and so she threw me that bone.

It was unfair that I had to negotiate right then. First I had to learn a way to think even when she was right in front of me. Breathe: in, out. Think.

"How could this work, Clare? Do you have a proposal?"

That last word hung ironically in the air. Her idea was the same as before. I would get uncontested custody of Kate. She and Anton would get Alexander's Woods. I wondered if she knew that Anton and his friends were threatening to put Lucky in jail in order to make this deal go over. I couldn't believe that she would be part of that.

"I don't think I should do that, Clare."

"You should have sold it years ago, Sam. Sold it or developed it yourself. Of course you couldn't do that because in your heart you want to pretend that you're a little boy playing in those woods, and that your Mommy is still alive."

"One thing I know, Clare. I would never trade my daughter for a piece of real estate."

The following day I had to take half the morning off to obey a subpoena from Mindy Faye, the lawyer for Randy Johnson's mother. Mrs. Johnson had already sued the school on account of her son's death.

"Yes, you have to come. It's a court order," Mindy explained. "Besides, we're on the same side. The school failed both of them, Kate and Randy both."

Kate's math teacher, Mr. Folsom, was in the teachers' lounge with me, also waiting to be deposed by Mindy Faye. He was scheduled to go first. I had never seen the man so agitated. His hair was longer and more disheveled than before. There were rings of sweat at the armpits of his dark print shirt.

"Mr. Alexander. You can see I'm upset about this. Would you mind very much ... Would you please go in first?"

"Yeah, sure." There were deep lines in his face, like he hadn't had any sleep in a long time. I remembered Kate saying that he always looked depressed, except when he was talking about math or the moon.

"What's the big deal?"

"You don't understand," Folsom whined. "They're not just suing the school. They're suing me too. They're saying I didn't supervise Randy Johnson correctly. They won't be satisfied until I'm hanging from a lamppost."

Chapter 24

I wish I could have been here yesterday when Mr. Folsom had his nervous breakdown or whatever it was. Maybe if there were another algebra person like me there, he wouldn't have gone off so bad. He tries to pretend he doesn't care that all the kids think algebra is such a joke. I'm just hoping he doesn't break down again.

So it's like a bad joke on me when he doesn't show up at all and Principal Freeland walks into the classroom instead. He is actually carrying an algebra book in his hand. They didn't come and get Lucky last night, but I don't know what's going to happen now.

"Everyone sit down please. Mr. Folsom is meeting with the school system's lawyers. We didn't have time to get a substitute. I'm going to take his place today. Can anybody show me last night's homework? Somebody tell me what chapter you're on."

He has to tell us again to sit down.

"Have you been doing anything at all in this class with Mr. Folsom?"

Mr. Folsom might be gay and a nervous wreck, but at least he really knows algebra. Freeland knows nothing but how to put the screws to us. Nobody answers him.

"I said, who can tell me what chapter you are on?" Freeland slams his book down on the teacher's desk.

In the dead silence that follows, Diane raises her hand. I hold my breath.

"If there is no asbestos in the school, why are you having it torn down?"

Diane, I'm thinking, this is a guy who can put people in jail.

"There was some fear of asbestos, but now it seems that there is none in the building. At the same time that we are looking at the insulation, we are also taking a look at the heating and cooling system. We are going to evaluate whether the systems are so old that the building has to be torn down anyway."

"So why did you already hire somebody to tear down the soccer stands?"

"My father," Lucky yells out, "told me he has it, the contract to tear down the soccer stands."

"Your father has a lot of problems, I hear. Like when the police arrested him for the murder of Randy Johnson and held him all night."

Lucky stands up.

Freeland puts his hands on his hips.

"We're on Chapter 17," I scream, looking at Lucky. Look at me, for God's sake. Look at me. Look at me. Yes.

"Earl," I'm on Diane's cell phone in the stall in the girls' room.

"Hi, honey."

"You have the contract to tear down the soccer stands?"

"Yeah."

"But that's all part of Anton's plan to tear down the woods and the school and everything?"

"Yeah. But it's a contract that I have."

"Lucky and I don't think you should do it."

"Then they'll just give the contract to somebody else."

"But can't you just pretend you're doing it, and not really do it?"

"You mean stall?"

"Yeah. Stall until ..."

"Until when, Kate?"

When we walk out of the last class, Corporal Walton is standing in the corridor. Lucky walks right up to him, holding his wrists together out in front.

"We don't need any cuffs for this chickenshit charge."

Chapter 25 ❧

Clare filed a petition to get custody of Kate, and I had to go to court. It was supposed to be just a scheduling conference, but I was afraid my weakness would poison even this. Clare, sitting at the other table in front of the judge's bench, actually gave me a little smile like we could work together at least on this little scheduling matter, but I tried not to get my hopes too high.

"Your Honor, we have reason to believe we might have an early settlement," Clare's lawyer started off. I looked over at John Murphy, my lawyer, but he was looking down at his calendar as if he hadn't heard. Had John made a deal without telling me? Could he do that? "If we can reschedule this scheduling conference for an hour from now, we believe we may have at least the broad outlines of a settlement to present to the court at that time."

"Fine, very good," the judge said. "In fact, I can make my jury room available to you for the next hour, if that would be of any help."

I turned to John Murphy in the hall.

"John, I don't get it. Is Clare giving up?"

His look obliterated all my hope. What kind of deal had he been forced to make, having a client like me?

"I was going to talk to you later about this."

"Is there a deal?"

"Come over here. Sit down. Okay. They just told me ten

minutes ago. They have new allegations."

"What does that mean?" I was pretty sure it meant that Clare, whether she smiled at me or not, was going to pound me and pound me until she beat me into a pulp.

"It's really ugly, and the way they're doing it ... I can't even help you. They know that too. I've got a trial in half an hour in Broward County. This here was supposed to be just a scheduling conference."

"You're not going in there with me?"

"I can't until late this afternoon, and that will be too late. These are reprehensible tactics they're using. It makes me ashamed of being a lawyer. I called my partner to see if he could sit in with you. But he's in a trial too. Let me explain what I can.

"Ethically, Clare's lawyer can't talk to you without me being there. But what he can do is file any papers he wants. He says he's going to file these really ugly allegations unless you talk them out of it right now. He knows I can't help you now." Murphy sighed. "You don't have to go in alone, but maybe you should go in there. It might be worth trying to talk them out of it."

"Why would I change my mind?"

"Maybe you should go in."

The jury room was painted white, with high windows up near the ceiling. There was a long table with chairs on both sides. Clare and her lawyer were sitting in the middle chairs at one long side, waiting. Clare looked up and caught my eye, and again I thought for a second she was happy to see me. Clare's lawyer, Preston, was beefy, middle-aged, bald, with a big square face and a dark moustache that looked like it belonged on a cartoon character. I felt like Clare wanted to say something personal to me first, maybe in private, but that he wouldn't let her.

"Mr. Alexander, my client and I want you to be aware of this additional pleading we have prepared, an emergency petition for her to obtain sole custody of your daughter. You should read it now."

"Why should I read it?"

"We are doing you a favor by asking you to read it first. You really ought to read it."

I took it from him. Clare avoided my eyes then. She was ashamed. I knew it was bad.

"What is this?" The first couple of pages, in their neat doubled-spaced type, just recited the facts of our marriage, such as the date, the place of marriage, the fact that we had a daughter, Kate. It was all true, but it was just the surface of our marriage that we showed to the outside world. This wasn't the real marriage between Sam and Clare.

"Keep reading." Preston reached across in front of Clare and helped me ruffle through a few pages until I got to the passages he wanted me to see.

"Petitioner hereby files this emergency petition for temporary custody based on the following emergency circumstances:

a. For approximately a year before the separation, Respondent Samuel Alexander displayed little or no normal marital interest in Petitioner, his wife and life partner.

b. At the same time, Petitioner displayed an unusual interest in their daughter Kate's development and became unusually close, kissing and hugging Kate in the presence of Petitioner to an extent not normal for the father of a girl in this stage of development.

c. Since the separation, Respondent has engaged in inappropriately close physical contact with Kate, admittedly causing himself to be sexually aroused by contact with his own daughter.

d. Respondent has admitted engaging in such contact

for the deliberate purpose of substituting such contact with his daughter for the sexual contact normally enjoyed between husband and wife."

"How could you!" I could only whisper. "You twisted every honest thing I said to you."

"e. As a direct result of Respondent's actions and admitted base and perverted intentions toward his daughter, said Kate is in imminent danger of immediate and irreparable harm if she is not immediately removed from Respondent's custody and control pending final resolution of this case."

I told Clare in the parking lot of Collins' restaurant that night about the moment – it was really only half a second – when I felt the warmth coming off Kate, and my body reacted like it was Clare in my arms. Afraid that something strange was happening to me, I pushed Kate away, hard. I told that story to Clare that night because I thought we were still friends. I thought if she knew how much I missed her, if she heard me humble myself so much, she might grant me a scrap of hope.

"Clare, this is really sick." My voice was back. "The only crime I committed that night with Kate was not holding on to her."

Clare still avoided my eyes. I enjoyed the shame she was feeling, and I wanted her to wallow in that shame right in front of me – and so I made her keep looking down at her hands. Preston understood everything, but he was perfectly willing to help Clare demean herself. I pushed up out of my chair and jumped over the table to go after him. I was across the table with my hand on his neck before the look on his face stopped me. What showed on his face right then, more than anything else, was patience. He was not ashamed of Clare. He was not ashamed of himself. He wasn't afraid, he wasn't angry, he wasn't upset, he wasn't surprised that I was going after him. He was just patiently waiting for it to be over with. I learned so much so fast from Preston's impassive eyes. I learned that no matter how horrible a crime Clare was committing against me and Kate right then, such crimes must be commonplace. They must be committed all the time. Preston was used to watching the agony of betrayed partners. He was comfortable with my outrage.

I pulled back. Preston the lawyer had not the slightest interest in whether anyone considered him a decent man. I could hurt him only physically, and there was no point in that.

"Clare, this is really sick of you."

"I'm only going by what Kate and you told me yourselves." But her voice was mechanical and small, and she avoided my eyes.

Preston interrupted. "Kate did confirm all the essential factual details. And it's not just Kate's word. Read the next paragraph."

"f. Petitioner has engaged an expert in child sexual abuse. Dr. Joan Blackwell, who, having interviewed the daughter, Kate, has opined that she suffers the obvious signs of post-traumatic stress caused by sexual abuse by her father, stress that may lead to severe life-long psychological symptoms if the child is not removed immediately from the custody of the abusing parent."

"So when did this woman interview Kate behind my back?"

"Last night."

"Kate was home all last night."

"On the phone." Preston sat back, straight-faced. "We might agree not to file these papers, but only if we can settle something here quickly. We have evidence to support these allegations at a hearing, if it ever has to get that far. My client will testify as to your admissions to her about ... your type of enjoyment of your contact with Kate. Kate's already told us the facts. It happened. The expert says it already caused her psychological damage. There's no chance that you'll get custody."

"Admit it, Clare. This is all about the woods."

"Listen, my client is willing not to file this petition, and not to reveal these allegations in open court, for all to see, in return for your agreeing to give the woods to her as a part of the final divorce agreement. If you agree right now, she will not file these papers and she will not fight you for custody of Kate."

"Clare, can you hear what he's saying? He's saying now that you think I'm abusing Kate, but that you don't really mind as long as I give you the woods. I'll tell you one thing, Clare. I can't wait to tell the judge about this."

"This is a settlement negotiation," Preston sharply corrected me. "Since it is a settlement negotiation, I can prevent you from testifying about anything that has been said in this room."

"Still, Clare, think. Now I have to tell Kate about what you're doing. Is that what you want?"

"Let me make one more thing perfectly clear," Preston interrupted again. "Once this petition is filed, together with our expert's report, it's doubtful you will ever be able to talk to Kate alone again."

What kind of father gets himself into a fix like this? I've done everything wrong, and Clare has played my bleating heart like some off-key instrument of torture.

"This is low, Clare. I know you want nothing to do with me. I can accept that. But you shouldn't do this to Kate. Not to yourself."

"To tell you the truth, Sam, I'm sick of feeling sorry for you."

"This could really hurt Kate."

"You said some weird things that night, Sam. Why would you say them if you didn't mean them?"

I didn't respond. I didn't want to debate points with her while she betrayed me. The pain of the knife in the back was enough. The cold light in the jury room that morning was perfect for dispelling illusions.

Chapter 26 ✑

"I don't know! I don't know why I talked to that woman, Dad. Get it? I don't know why I screwed up everybody's life. I just did it."

She ran up the stairs and slammed the door to her bedroom. I would have let it go at that, but lawyer Preston's words echoed in my mind. I went up after her and barged in.

"Kate, they tell me that I may never be able to talk to you alone after this court hearing."

"Dad, I'm sorry."

"I don't need you to be sorry. I need you to talk to me now, because this might be the last conversation we ever have."

"They can't really do that to us, can they?"

"They can. Things have consequences. Kate, if there's anything you want to say to me, or if there's anything you want explained, now's the time to do that."

She lifted her head up from the pillow. "Dad, I'm sorry. That woman called, real friendly. I didn't say anything bad about you. Just a couple of minutes."

"What did she ask?"

"About me. Do I have a 'satisfying relationship' with a boyfriend. I said yes, but she already knew he's in jail. She made me talk about what Johnson did to me and why I let it happen the second time. Then she asked if I ever touched a girl, and I said yes, and then she didn't even ask what kind of touching, if it was just a hug or whatever. She hung up right after that."

"Why didn't you tell me?"

"Because she made me feel like such a retarded slut. I know I screwed up again. I always screw everything up."

"She's writing some kind of report that I had sexual contact with you and it's too dangerous for you to keep living here."

She sat up and stared at me through her tears.

"Why do people do things like this?" She was looking at me but her eyes were focused somewhere in between the two of us, as if the answer would be found there.

"Because we let them."

I have to see her, even if I have to walk through the woods alone to get there. The dogs are here, wriggling against me on the back deck. The puppies' eyes are open now, seeing everything for the first time. Take a good look and enjoy it before it all turns to shit. Rudi finally comes to the door wearing a green terrycloth robe that splits to show her long legs every time she moves, fuzzy yellow mules and a pink towel wrapped around her head like a turban. We sit at the kitchen table. She's so much taller than me and she sits so naturally straight that I have to look up to meet her eyes. Water drips down her face from under the towel, and she pulls the towel off and dries her hair with it, one side at a time, as we talk.

"Men love you, don't they? You must spend every minute you're not in a bar working on your hair or your skin or your figure."

She stops drying her hair. Her voice is tiny.

"When a man says you're beautiful, it just means he wants something."

"You just get off on getting men hot, don't you? Even fourteen-year-olds. Now Lucky's bound to think about you forever."

She closes her eyes. Her face looks awful.

"You could go to jail."

"I'm not afraid of jail. I've been put away before. When I was twelve. When I was a lot dumber even than I am now."

She puts her face down in her hands.

"I thought, when I first met Earl, I could be better."

"You're not." I'm thinking there are so many disguises people use to hide the meanness inside. They can be evil even if they are drop dead gorgeous or talk like a principal. Or if they are your mother.

"Back then I was really mad at Earl. He was working all the time, never here. He wouldn't let me go out by myself. He was hounding me to quit my job. I've walked out on plenty of men before, but I just couldn't walk away from Earl. He was holding me here. He was holding me here, but he was never here himself, and he had me so hot and mixed up and pissed off that I would have done anything to get free. I would have killed him if I was the kind of person that could kill. So I did the next best thing, the only kind of killing I know how to do."

"I hate you."

"I saw that sweet young boy come up here all the time so lonely, and I wanted to make him shake, make him die to be with me."

My own legs are shaking as I stand up to run.

"I'm calling the police. You are so evil."

"No!"

She grabs me and holds me so tight I can't even move my arms. She's really strong. I try to get away but we fall down and she's on top of me. She's trying to talk to me at the same time, and her face is so close I can smell her lavender conditioner. Her turban is gone and her long hair is dripping on my face. Don't, she keeps saying, don't.

"Listen, Kate. I know I got this mean streak in me. It comes out sometimes."

"Tell me about it."

"And since this mean streak came out even after Earl loved me, I figure it ain't ever going away. Most of the things I did to men in the past were things they probably had coming. But now, I got real nice people around me I don't want to hurt, but that meanness still comes out."

"Evil bitch."

"These men all think I'm so stupid, Kate. I knew all about their stupid gun. That night that poor boy was shot, I heard it of course. I knew it was Earl's .357. When I heard that shot, I thought it was Lucky, doing it to himself. I thought it was me who made him do it.

"That's really why they put me away as a kid, Kate. It happened to me as a kid, with my uncle – only I was younger, only twelve. It happened every week, sometimes two or three times a week, but I never knew when it was going to happen. I was scared all the time, and all the time I went around ... I was so dirty. One day after he got off of me I took all the pills in the house, even the horse pills from the stable. They had to stick me in the hospital and pump my stomach. They never let me come back home for a year."

She lets me go, but I'm listening now. She's crying, her face is all wet and her eyes are red and swollen, and it's hard to believe she was ever pretty.

"The night that shot went off in the woods, I sat out there on the deck, just waiting to hear that Lucky was dead, and thinking. I sat out there until after midnight, until I found out it wasn't Lucky who got shot."

I'm staring at her, wondering why I'm not hating her. I'm still crying when I think about what she took from me.

"Lucky," I say, "whenever he's kissing me or anything, all he's going to be thinking about is you."

"No." She's wiping her eyes on her robe, shaking her head. "Listen. I know a lot more about guys than you do, Kate. When guys get so hot, honest to God, they'll do it with anything that has a hole between its legs. That's what Lucky acts like when he's around me now, like I'm a hole that he stuck himself into one time when he was out of his mind."

"You're still hanging around. You're still teasing him."

"No. No. I'm not doing that now, honey."

"You do it without even knowing you're doing it."

"I love both of those guys. That's the best man and the best boy I ever saw."

"All you do is hurt them. You are just a hole."

I can't believe I said that. She looks at me like a beat-up, twelve-year-old girl.

"My mother always told me I was good for nothing but hurting all the people around me. I got to admit. She was right."

Chapter 27

Ms. Nesbitt sprayed on a little too much Final Net, and the mounds of stiff red curlicues pointing in all directions make her freckled white face look so small. She is walking back and forth, waiting for the last kid to sit down, her eyes looking far off somewhere. She's been quiet for the last week. I thought it was because of Johnson being killed. Lucky told me last week she doesn't care about the school any more because she's being fired anyway.

"Can anyone tell me what the word 'transmutation' means?"

No one knows, but the question shuts everybody up. Ms. Nesbitt holds her head perfectly still, but her eyes are looking all around the room. When she is like this, it means she is going to make us listen.

"Transmutation is the changing of one substance into another, by magic. That's what the Alchemists tried to do in medieval times. By means of magic, they tried to change ordinary metals into gold.

"Now," she raps hard on the desk with a pointer, "why should we care about transmutation in this school, in this modern age?

"Because," she answers herself, "because transmutation has happened in Glenwood. According to Principal Freeland, it has occurred right in the walls of this building. According to Principal

Freeland, harmless fiberglass insulation suddenly transmuted itself into dangerous asbestos just this year.

"There definitely," her eyes dart around the room, "was only fiberglass before, and yet Freeland told the whole school there was asbestos."

What gets everybody's attention is her saying "Freeland" without saying "Principal."

"So, one of the following must be true. Either," she points both hands, palms up, toward the door, "fiberglass has been transmuted into asbestos, or," she swings her arms and points the other way, "Principal Freeland has told us a lie.

"It's one," she says, swinging her arms toward the door again, "or the other," shifting back the other way. "Not both.

"We are going to have a special class about this. I had thought that this was a rather simple concept, but now I see that everyone in this school, including the principal, needs to learn to appreciate how rare it is that a transmutation takes place."

"There's not supposed to be any more outdoor classes."

"I'm making an exception."

"Won't you get fired?"

Ms. Nesbitt doesn't answer.

"Everybody says the whole school's going to be torn down anyway," some kid yells out. "So who cares?"

"You need to care." Her voice echoes in the room. "You need to learn, no matter what buildings are torn down or where you may go next year, that it matters if you are lied to."

"Dude," Diane whispers to me. "Like everyone doesn't already know he always lies."

"So what we're going to do is have a special class. It will be called the Celebration of the Chemical Transmutation of Fiberglass into Asbestos. It's going to be held outside tomorrow in the soccer stands. Everyone should bring a chemistry book, or an alchemy book, or a book about magic. Or you can dress like a sorcerer, or a witch ... or a swindler. And there's a homework assignment. I want everyone to be prepared to have an opinion about whether chemical transmutation has happened right here in our school – or, if it wasn't transmutation, exactly what happened."

Some parents are afraid to let their kids go outside the school now, but I know all the kids will go. What gets me is she thinks this one lie makes so much difference.

Ms. Nesbitt's curls are a lot looser the day the Transmutation class is supposed to happen, but her face is tighter.

"I have been informed by Principal Freeland that I am not allowed to hold the outdoor class today."

"What? After we made our costumes and all?" Diane doesn't even have a costume. I look at her.

Ms. Nesbitt taps the end of a pencil into the palm of her hand. While she's doing this, we all see Freeland step into the doorway. She taps the pencil slower.

"Excuse me, Principal Freeland," she walks toward him. "We're going for our outdoor class now. And students, I need to tell you that this is an unauthorized class, and I am being suspended from my job for holding it, so anyone who is afraid to follow me outside can stay here in the room." At the last second Freeland steps aside.

"Let's be honest about a few things." Ms. Nesbitt uses a megaphone. "There never was any asbestos in the school building. The people who built the building thirty years ago knew this. The people who replaced the heating system three years ago knew it. Principal Freeland knew it.

"I never tried to be like the other teachers. I never tried to explain everything to you all the time. I figured you needed to see things with your own eyes. But you have to look. Really look. Then you can figure things out for yourself.

"I think you can. So let's look. So come on down out of the stands now, all you alchemists and sorcerers, swindlers and card sharks and flim-flam artists, and see if you can transmute one material thing into another. And if you can't, then you will be able to see with your own eyes that something is not right, and that we have among us a person of high authority who wrongfully claims that he can do what no mortal can do."

It's pretty much chaos from then on. Some kids are marching and strutting in costumes, swirling capes and pretending to say magic words, but most of us are sitting in the stands, gossiping. Somebody says Ms. Nesbitt doesn't want to be a teacher anyway.

I decide to tell Diane what my father has supposedly done to me. Before I can, she grabs my arm and pulls me away from the other kids in the stands. She takes a deep breath.

"It's about Carl."

"What's up with Carl?"

I figure Carl has left her. It should be so simple: you should be with the people you love. Why does it almost never happen? She sobs in my arms.

"Carl's gone?"

She snorts, pulls herself together, blows her nose.

"No, he's here all right. But I'm pregnant."

Right then, machines start arriving, I guess to take down the fence or the stands. A big construction machine with a huge claw hanging off the front of it drives off the back of a truck and towards us. It wiggles forward, crossing the filled-in ditch at the end of the field, then stops. The driver climbs down, leaving the motor spitting out little clouds of black smoke into the air, and walks toward us. He's wearing a baseball cap and big sunglasses. A girl in a black sequined dress and a witch's hat tries to show him her long purple fingernails, and he pretends to smile. A tall boy in a top hat hits him in the face with a balloon. Then I see the reddish-grey sideburns. It's Earl.

"You're all going to have to move out. I got a contract to tear down those stands. Got to be done by the end of the day."

202

"Earl. Hi! It's me."

"Oh. Hi, honey. I can't stall any longer. I got a urgent call from the county."

"It's not the county. It's Anton, and you know it." I'm screaming. "And you're helping him. I thought you were one of the good guys. "

"Sorry, honey."

I run and sit on the claw of his machine. It's dirty and the metal is really cold. He jumps off and runs around to pull me off.

"Don't you dare touch that student." Ms. Nesbitt.

"Kate, you gotta have some common sense. They've already paid me a lot of money ..."

"I'm telling Lucky. I'm telling Lucky. Even if I have to get put in jail just so I can talk to him. You're a part of all this shit, Earl!"

After school, Mr. Folsom sits down across from me in the classroom. Both elbows are on his desk and he's running both of his shaky hands through his hair.

"Why didn't you come to class this morning?"

He just keeps pulling at his hair like he has a terrible headache.

"What's the use? They're forcing me to go back to the deposition and answer all their questions. If I refuse, I'll be fired."

"Why don't you just do it?"

"I'm afraid, okay? To talk. They can ask you anything. Did you know that? And you have to answer? You're a smart girl, Kate. You know what they're going to ask me about. All about. Every detail."

"They can't ask you ..."

"Oh yes they can. They're asking everybody about their personal sex life. Randy had a sex problem, so they can ask all

203

of us about that."

"But really, nothing will happen if they find out, will it?"

"Kate, there have been campaigns, in this state, in this county, to get rid of openly gay teachers."

"Couldn't you fight that?"

"I lost it in class the other day. I told the kids to forget about school, that it was full of lies. I didn't mean it. I believe that everybody needs school; everybody needs to learn. Especially you, Kate. You need to keep trying to learn no matter how oppressive this place gets."

"If it weren't for the principal, this might be a good school."

"It really shouldn't matter to you how dishonest the principal is. The only way they can beat you is if you give up and quit learning."

"But why are you going to let them beat *you*?"

His hands are out of his hair. They're shaking. He puts one hand on top of the other and tries to hold both down on top of his desk.

"I'm never going to the moon, Kate."

"Why?"

"I'm not … the kind of person people want. They're going to make me answer all kinds of questions. They're blaming me for everything. They're going to smoke me out and get rid of me."

The night Johnson was killed, after Lucky and I heard the shot, and after we heard someone running back up the trail, I poked my head up and looked, even though Lucky said it was dangerous. It was Mr. Folsom.

Chapter 28

I met Earl at a restaurant and bar on Glenwood's three-block commercial street, the same street his office backed up to. The place was kind of a compromise. There was no tablecloth or wine list, but there also wasn't a jukebox or any muddy footprints on the floor. As soon as we sat down, Earl called out to the waitress. By the time she was finished taking our order, Earl had brought the sparkle back to her eyes.

"It's too easy for you, Earl."

"Yeah, they always like me. All the same, it ain't done me much good."

"You know a lot more about women than I do."

Earl sat back and crossed one muddy boot at the knee.

"So why are we here?"

"I want you to tell me what to do," I said. Earl ran his finger back and forth through a sideburn, tilting himself back in his chair. "It's Clare. You know that she left me for Anton. It was rough, but I'm getting over it. No, I mean it. I'm getting over her. But I saw something really funny, and I wonder what you think I should do."

"What did you see?"

"At work I usually don't go out to lunch, but my boss and I were in a good mood yesterday and we went out to this big lunch place near the county office building. I saw Anton at a table. He wasn't with Clare. He was with another woman. I know. I know what you're going to say. He takes all kinds of people to lunch. He's a salesman by trade. But, you know, Earl, I could see what he was selling."

"You want to tell Clare?"

"Not because I want her back. Not after what she's done."

Earl's chair tipped back again.

"Should I tell her? I mean, I'm not thinking about me. I'm resigned to the fact that I'm over here and she's over there and that's the way it's going to be. But I do care about her – as a person, I mean. I don't want to see her humiliated."

"You're not like me," Earl said, taking a swig from his bottle and looking at me out of the corner of his eye like he didn't want to let such a suspicious character out of his sight. "I can see your mind's coming up with sneaky ways to keep some kind of hold on her."

"I'm just concerned. I'm worrying about a friend getting herself hurt."

"You're full of shit."

Uh. Okay. "Every time I think I've turned a corner, she just gets to me again. It's the same thing over and over. I'm telling you, my mind is twisted around her like DNA."

"Thinking about her ain't gonna help."

The waitress came back to our table, expecting Earl to turn on the charm again, but he wasn't in the mood.

"I envy all you know about women, Earl."

He was actually drinking slower than I.

"Rudi's the one made me see how much I was drinking. She made me cut down a lot on that, but now it's happening again."

"Drinking more now?"

He looked at the rerun of some football game on the giant TV and made eye contact with a woman a few tables down from us. I kept staring at him, a little numb in the face from drinking myself, until he answered.

"I got a funny effect on women. They love the hell out of me at first, then it proceeds to them hating me. The middle part is when they use all kind of excuses to get out of the house."

"You think she's cheating on you?"

He winked at the waitress and she brought him another beer.

"Naw. If it was just that, I'd just kick her pretty ass out. I'm just not enough for her now. I don't know what it is."

The Rudi I saw definitely seemed in love with Earl; but then, what did I know about women?

"Hey, you got one firecracker of a daughter! Put the screws to me! I got a contract to tear down the school soccer stands. I had a backhoe out there. Damn if that little bitch didn't sit her ass right on it until I had to back off."

"You have a contract with Anton?"

"The county."

"Same thing."

"Thing is, this is costing me money."

"She's a great kid."

"One more woman helping me do right for a while. If they'd all give up on me, I'd be a lot drunker and a lot richer."

The waitress brought him a cup of coffee and we watched the game for a while.

"Almost forgot! Listen to this! The police come to my house with a search warrant today. Chopped down the bird house. Took it away."

"A warrant for a bird house?"

"And the steel pole it was settin' on. See, that's where we kept our gun. That kid was shot with our gun."

"Your gun?"

He nodded. "Yeah. But I talked to the cops all night the night it happened. Cleared the air and all. They don't think it was me or Lucky. They want to see who else put their hands on that birdhouse."

Chapter 29

They make me sit outside the courtroom so I can't hear my mother talking about what a whore I am. By the time I go in everybody will know it. My father's lawyer sends somebody to sit with me in that hall. Dave is much younger than Dad. He looks like he's trying to look like a lawyer, with a starched white shirt and a blue tie. He has a round face and glasses. He sits a ways away, probably because he's too scared to sit next to a slut like me.

"So it's your job," I say, "to keep me from running away?"

"No." He does not look at me. "I guess I'm supposed to make you feel more comfortable while you're waiting to testify."

"From over there?"

He gets up and sits in the chair next to me. "I'm sorry. I'm new at this." He's so stiff, and his suit is so clean, he looks like he would never do anything wrong or even understand why anyone would.

"Can people just go in there and lie? Can they just go in there like my mother is and make up horrible stuff, and nothing happens to them for lying?"

"I don't really know that much about it yet," he says. "I guess you should just tell the truth, and it'll be okay. That's the whole idea of how it's supposed to work anyway."

"Do you know what they're saying about me?"

"You seem like a nice girl to me."

"I look like a nice person, but I might be a whore, right?"

"I believe you. So will the judge, I think."

They open this giant wooden door and call my name. Inside, Dad looks like Mom has punched him in the stomach and he's trying not to give her the pleasure of seeing him puke. My mother meets my eyes, holding her neck stiff, her witch eyes glinting. I'm sure she already told everyone that I was groping Dad or something.

Dad is such a wimp. After all she's done to him, his eyes still go foggy and his voice catches whenever he talks about her. Of course you can't blame him for loving his wife, but come on – *after* she runs out on you in front of the whole town and *then* says you were messing with your own daughter? Grow a pair, Dad. But to be fair, he's in this mess right now because he loves me too. Mom can't accept that. His loving me at all is the worst insult of all to her.

Dad's lawyer talked to me earlier. "You mother's lawyer, Preston, will be asking you questions. He is not going to try to get you to say that you had ... incestuous relations with your father." He was calm, and he looked me in the eye, but those heavy words almost knocked the wind out of me. I could feel my face turning red. "It won't be anything like that at all. He is just going to try to get you to say that you hugged your Dad that night – and there is certainly nothing wrong with that. It's the truth, from what you told me. What he wants you to say is that you were confused by the way that he touched you, or that he acted strange, or that he was breathing funny – anything like that."

"Oh."

"So the best thing to do is stick to the facts. And be definite. I mean, don't let him trick you into saying you were confused by what your father was doing, if you weren't."

But I am confused. That night, Dad was watching TV in the dark because he was so lonely. Then I hugged him so tight he must have gotten turned on. I'm the one who caused it. Maybe I did it on purpose because I really am a twisted little slut like Mom is saying. Maybe I'm the lowest kind of slut, one who does her dirt without even knowing it, somebody who acts all nice on the outside, where people can see, but who is rotten inside. They're making me show my own rotten soul in court so everybody can see. But the worst thing is, I will have to keep looking at my own soul from now on, all the time, forever. If I could take a pill and die right now I would.

I don't even hear the first few questions.

"Miss?" It's the judge, leaning toward me. He's bald, but he looks like he hasn't condemned me yet. He reminds me of Dave, the assistant lawyer who was with me outside in the hall, who told me just to say the plain truth. Dave said that the plain truth couldn't hurt me. I'm sure it can't hurt good people like him, but it might hurt me.

"Did you hear the question?" The judge's voice is gentle.

"No."

Then I answer a couple of easy questions.

"So," lawyer Preston harrumphs. He looks like the Walrus in Alice in Wonderland. He finishes all his soft, butter-me-up questions. He finishes making me admit some plain things, such as where I was on different nights when, he pretends, my mother was looking for me.

"So you were in the dining room in the dark with your father, hugging him?'"

My mother believes it at least a little bit or she wouldn't do this to me. She wants to prove in court what a sick slut I am. How much lower I am than her. Why I am such trash she was glad to leave me. Dad has this sick look in his eyes too.

Assistant lawyer Dave catches my eye and moves his hand like he's drinking a glass of water. I reach for the glass in front of me. Then Dad's lawyer stands up and says "I object," just like on television. Then the lawyers argue with the judge for a while.

I drink all the water I can stand while they wait for me. How about a little help, Dad, instead of looking down at your shoes? I look over at assistant lawyer Dave's eyes again. He's trying to look like he believes in me.

The judge finally settles the argument, and lawyer Preston begins asking me questions with this look on his face like he's caught me having sex with a dog or something. And that really makes me mad, because there's no way he could know. I glance over at Mom and it hits me that she doesn't know either. She's just pretending she knows, and that is *really* sick. Her face looks pinched and she doesn't seem either beautiful or scary to me now. I look at Dave, the assistant lawyer. There is really no way he could know either. I am the only one who knows the truth about what happened.

"So, this scene started with you hugging your father, very tightly, in the living room, in the dark?"

Dad's lawyer objects again, and there's another argument. I'm not going to lie about any of the little pieces of what happened, or what I did. Everybody knows all that anyway. So then I'm thinking, like, why are we here? So the judge can decide? How would he know?

The judge decides that Preston can ask his question.

"So the scene started with you hugging your father, very tightly, in the living room, in the dark."

"No, that's not how it started. He was by himself, in the dark, with the TV on, watching the news. That's how it started."

"But then you hugged him very closely, pulling your bodies tightly together, didn't you?"

"He did that every night – stared at either the TV or the wall. I could hardly get him to even answer me. He was so sad after Mom left that I was afraid that he'd like go into a deep hole and never come out."

"So you hugged him really closely, pulling your bodies tightly together?"

"Everybody knows that. What you're asking is, was I trying to get him hot. No. Not on purpose. Not any other way."

"Fine. I will accept that your intentions were pure, totally pure. But that doesn't say anything about your father's intentions. You couldn't really know, could you, what your father's intentions were?"

"I guess not."

After that, they let me sit outside the courtroom, alone this time. I sit alone now because, once I finished testifying, it doesn't matter to them if I run away or not. After a while though, Dave comes out and sits down right next to me. He looks a little freaked out.

"What's happening in there?"

"Expert. They just heard the testimony of Dr. Blackwell, the expert witness."

"So, what'd she say?"

"The worst possible stuff. About you, and your father. About how it would be dangerous for you to ever be alone with him."

"We already knew she was going to say that. She called me on the phone real late one night and asked me about ten questions and wouldn't let me answer and hung up on me."

"Mr. Murphy knew that her whole report was based on that one phone interview. He established that pretty well on cross-examination. I hope I can cross examine that well one day, but ..."

"... the judge believes her anyway?"

"I don't know if he believes her or not. She got paid $10,000 for making that one phone call and testifying against you in court. She doesn't know you even as well as I do, but her opinion counts a thousand times more than anybody else's. I just didn't know before now how this system really works."

They let me come in again for the decision.

"There has not been much concrete evidence presented today

that anything improper at all occurred between Mr. Alexander and his daughter, Kate. It's possible that there was nothing more here than a father and daughter comforting each other, or at least trying to comfort each other, at a time of great stress. But the testimony of Ms. Blackwell concerns me quite a lot. Ms. Blackwell is one of the world's foremost experts on child abuse, having testified in over a hundred cases nationwide in the past two years alone. Her testimony is that Kate has already suffered serious psychological consequences from her recent contact with her father and that Kate's condition will continue to deteriorate as long as she continues to dwell in the same house as her father.

"Admittedly, there's not a lot of hard evidence to back up that opinion, but it is the opinion of a renowned expert in the field. I have to give that opinion some credit. The court thus finds that the welfare of the child is at imminent risk while she dwells with her father, and also finds that there is a quite viable alternative, transfer of sole custody to the mother, which would pose no risk to anyone, and which would bring no danger of anyone losing his rights in the long run. So, as an emergency order, and until this court can set up a date for a full custody hearing, which should be sometime within the next sixty days, I am awarding temporary custody to the mother.

"Father is prohibited from having any unsupervised contact with the child."

Chapter 30

The witch drives me back to get my clothes and waits outside in the car. Coming down the stairs with my stuff, I turn into the kitchen. I know I can escape out the side door and run away, but I don't. I swear, I've done a lot of stupid things, but I've never done anything stupider than what that judge just did.

"So, what's this, the parking lot for the apartment you pretend to live in?"

"Pretend?"

"Yeah, while you're shacking up with Anton, getting high off his checkbook and his chemical suntan?"

She doesn't say anything.

"You lost the case," I say.

"I won, at least temporarily. You're with me, aren't you?"

"You didn't want me."

She stretches out her neck a little like she always does when she is telling herself she's right.

"How can you say that? I wanted you. I was worried about you."

She looks straight out the window, breathing through her mouth. Then she sighs and the lines of her face soften. She looks over at me in the way she always does when she's informing people that she is right. She slowly turns her head, opens her eyes wide and focuses them on you. She knows she's pretty and those eyes will make you believe her.

"Listen, Kate, You have to believe me. Your father can't let go of me. He's pretending to himself that I'm not gone. I can't tell you all the details, but he was getting you and me confused in his mind."

"I'm the one your lawyer called a slut in court today."

She closes her eyes. "I didn't mean for that to happen."

"But it's what you think, isn't it?"

Her apartment is on the second level of a three-story complex surrounding a parking lot. We walk up concrete stairs to her level. Her living/dining room opens onto a tiny concrete balcony overlooking the grounds of a nursing home.

"Why did you bother?"

"What?" She looks at me sourly.

"Why did you bother to rent this? Everybody knows you're living with Anton in his father's old house in Wood Park."

"I live here." Her voice is icy. "I want to show you the rest."

She walks me down a short hall, picking up speed. She points out a mirror with a fake bamboo brass frame and a blond, kidney shaped coffee table that I'm sure nobody will ever be allowed to put a coffee cup on. She swivels her shoulders as she points out the closets and the new carpet. She's doing her real estate act.

"Here's my bedroom." It's kind of plain. The wallpaper is a vague beige with a pattern of really thin gold lines. "See, I took the duvet and the bureau from our house. Just some things to remind me of the home we had."

"What's over here?" I'm still standing in the hall, looking at another doorway.

"It's the second bedroom." We go to the door. The room is even plainer.

"Why did you get two bedrooms? Does Anton come over and sleep in a separate bedroom?"

She goes back into her bedroom and sits down on the bed.

"I can see this is not going to be easy. I thought it might be fun, the two of us getting together, at least for a while."

"The three of us, you mean? Isn't Anton included? Or are you going to go fuck him somewhere else?"

"Kate, it's your Dad."

I'm standing in my sleeping T-shirt near the phone in Mom's living room. Behind the sliding glass doors to the balcony two giant trees on the nursing home grounds form a canopy of leaves that glow yellow in the early sunlight. Those two trees are so beautiful it makes me sad to watch them, the way they are so alone and so set apart in that manicured lawn.

"It's your Dad."

I stare at her until she leaves.

"Dad. Why did you say those idiot things to Mom?"

"Not everything I've said since your mother left has made complete sense."

"You got that right."

"I tried to take care of you."

"Look where I am now, Dad."

He said I had to go to be questioned by Lawyer Faye, at school.

"Oh. Johnson. Like the thing that Mr. Folsom is so freaked out about."

"That very thing."

"Will they ask me if I've been groping my own father?"

"I've kicked myself a million times for the way I told it to your mother. I'm so sorry, Kate."

"That night, I didn't feel like I was doing anything wrong."

"You didn't do anything wrong, Kate."

"I'm sorry I talked to that bitch of a shrink."

"That's not your fault. It didn't matter what you said. No matter what you said to her, she would've still written that same report."

"I hate it here, Dad. Isn't there anything we can do so I can come back?"

There's like a real long pause, and then Dad's voice sounds like he's talking to someone else. "Mr. Murphy says I have to hire a psychologist too."

"Dad, can't you help *now*? This is awful!"

"There is one thing, Kate, but I don't know if it would be right."

Earl calls me almost every day after school to whine about me sitting on his bulldozer or whatever that thing was.

"They put your son in jail." I tell him every time. Actually, I hope this doesn't get him so pissed that he stops calling, because usually I can get him to say something about Lucky. Earl says Lucky's doing okay and doesn't really seem to mind it that much. He never says that Lucky asked about me.

Mr. Folsom is back, his hair now cut smooth in a strange pageboy look. I can feel how desperate he is to fit in, and I wish I could just tell him to give it up. I corner him after class.

"They're making me answer questions today about Johnson," I start off.

"The lawyers?"

"I guess to prove I led Johnson on or something."

"Jesus Christ!"

"No. Mindy Faye."

"How do things get so ... twisted around?" He pulls on his fingers.

"I do feel bad about things I said to him, you know, on his very last day."

"Don't feel guilty, Kate. He was a predator. People in the school willed themselves not to see that."

"I saw you that night. Running out of the woods. I never told anybody. Not the police. Not even Lucky."

"Why not?"

"Even if you did it, I wouldn't tell."

"What are you saying? You think I'd murder that boy?"

"Even if you did do it, I wouldn't tell."

"I didn't do it," he screams. "You're the one person I thought had faith in me." Then he stands up, walks around me and stomps out of the room.

I'm probably the last person who talked to Randy Johnson before he died. I can't tell anybody about it. It's so ugly I can't get it out of my mind. I'd never seen anybody jerking off, and it was totally gross, with him calling out my name faster and faster. He didn't even take his hands off his thing when I came up close.

"Kate."

"Get away from me!"

"I love you."

"If you touch me, I swear I'm going to knock your thing off with this stick."

I walked behind him on the bridge and he didn't move. I made it past him to the path, but he was still looking at me.

"I love you."

I ran back and hit him in the face really hard. He screamed and slumped over. Then he cried for so long I was sorry for doing that. His face was bleeding and his whole body was shaking. I was still holding the stick and waiting – I don't know what for. After a long time, he stopped crying and shaking and sobbing. He wasn't playing with himself, but he didn't pull up his pants either. He didn't have any pride. He didn't have anything. He looked up at me again.

"I love you, Kate."

"No. You can't love me."

"I love you, Kate."

I dropped the stick. It wasn't enough.

Chapter 31

"Listen, honey. Every day, the Director of Public Works for the county calls me and asks why the soccer stands aren't torn down yet."

And then, every day, Earl calls me. I'm just back from school, sitting in my mother's dining "area." It's not really an actual room. I'm looking out through the glass door to the balcony. I've never lived in an apartment before, and it's weird that your feet don't touch the ground when you go out the door. Even when you go down the steps outside all you get to is a parking lot. Mom has decorated it okay, if you like her real-estate-model-home style, but it feels like I'm living in a box.

"What about Lucky? Can't you get him out? Is he okay?"

"He's doing all right. Nobody messes with him any more. The guards aren't a whole lot better than the kids, he says. He's friends with some of the kids."

"He's like – what? – *getting used to it?*"

"Seems like."

He never says Lucky asked about me.

"What you're saying now is you're going to do it, tear down the soccer stands to help Anton, because that's what the county school people are paying you money to do."

"I got no choice. I got a contract."

My mother's so hooked on Anton she's not herself. She didn't tell me Anton's coming here, and she didn't tell him either that I would be here when he comes. His wasted eyes go big when he sees me open the door. Something is different about those dyed blonde curls tonight. Mom gushes all over him, puts her hands on him, pulls him in. Even he's embarrassed.

"Talk in the bedroom," he orders her, then slouches down the hall. Mom teeters off balance after him, dragged along I guess by his charisma and his manly cologne, but pulling on his shirtsleeve like a little kid.

"No ... um ... no, Anton. Please, the living room, please."

He stops.

"I want you to get to know Kate."

"I already know him," I say.

"Yeah. Hi, Kate. Hey, you mind if your mother and I talk to each other alone in the living room a little bit?"

I go into the kitchenette and make myself a little pizza in the toaster oven. I don't hear them talking, and the lights are off. Anton's keys scrape across the coffee table. I pull out the pizza too soon, and it's half done and tastes awful. I pour myself a soda with ice and wait for the fizzing to die down. I'm sitting there boiling over and I don't know what to do, and I decide I'm just going to do whatever Lucky would do.

He's all over my mother on the sofa. She's breathing hard and pretending to push his hands away. I flick on the lights.

"Hey! Mind if I sit down? Is this like a reality show?"

"I thought you had some sense," Anton growls. He gets up like he's coming after me, and I run back to my room. I don't know if he's really coming after me or not. I'm breathing hard and the lights are off. Soon I can see there's a faint light at my window. No moon, but the stars are brilliant.

The door opens. Thank God it's Mom's silhouette.

"Mom, you still have your clothes on!"

I can almost make out her features.

Anton's shadow glides up beside her, puts his arms around

her waist. I know what Diane would say right now.

"Mom, can I ask you a question? It's a personal question about you and Anton."

"Of course, honey. This is a tough situation for you. I'll try to answer anything. I haven't been the perfect mother, I know. At least I can try to be straightforward with you."

"Okay. So Mom, when you're in bed with Anton, and he gets naked, and he takes off his wig, is the dome of his head white, or is it that gross artificial tan like his face?"

"There's a hearing this morning in juvenile court about your friend Lucky."

She's making me breakfast.

"What? How do you know?"

"I promise you, Kate. I still don't have any idea why they put him in jail."

"Oh, come on, Mom. Freeland *told me*. You think I'm so stupid."

"I never thought ... I can't believe that Anton had anything to do with that."

"Freeland told me three times, Mom. He even called me at Diane's. All the charges against Lucky will be dropped as soon as you and Anton get the property."

"We really need that property, but no one would do that. Anton has his faults, Kate, but he is not a cruel person."

"Faults? You mean like cheating Carl's father out of his money?"

"Kate, don't assume that Anton cheated somebody just because some business deal went wrong."

"Or the hundred other women in Glenwood that he fucked?"

This stops her for a second. "You're growing up faster than you should, Kate. Okay. I know that Anton had his wild days. Those days are over now, Kate. Hopefully, he's found what he needed in me."

"Is that why his secretary Mrs. Rose told me just last summer never to be alone with him in a model home?"

Dad shows up at school to take me to Lucky's hearing. He looks so worried and pathetic in his Little Boy Blue slacks, his yellow shirt and blue tie, making a fist with one hand and holding it with the other like a ball as he looks for me in the corridor.

"Daddy!" I say extra loud, hugging and squeezing him. "This is my Daddy!" I say to a kid walking by. I don't know why. Maybe because I can't stand the way he acts. He acts like he's afraid to touch me.

"Cut it out, Kate."

I'm crying on the way to the car.

"It's only temporary, Kate. I'm doing everything I can."

"I hate it at Mom's, Dad. I hate you. You're acting like the judge was right."

We go into a little room in the courthouse. Dad's lawyer, Murphy, is going to be Lucky's lawyer too. He was nice to me the day Mom made me testify. He smiles when I walk in with Dad.

"There *were* two charges, the pot smoking and the handgun charges. It seems the police lost the marijuana test results. Very unusual. I've never seen this happen before. The pot smoking charges are out the window. The handgun charge is the more serious charge."

"Yeah?"

"They did find Lucky's fingerprints on that gun. But, I don't know how many courtroom movies you've seen. Fingerprints can last for months, and they're having trouble proving that Lucky touched that gun *after* he was on probation."

"Yeah?"

"That's why they subpoenaed you here, to make you testify as to when Lucky touched that gun."

"I won't."

"Oh. Well, Kate, I have to tell you that they theoretically can hold you in contempt if you refuse to testify. The judge can put you in the detention center immediately, and he can keep you there until you will talk."

"Then I guess it's my turn."

Sometimes, just the way certain guys look at you can make you feel pretty, or funny, or smart. The way Murphy looks at me now, it's not any of those things, but I am eating up the way he is looking at me.

"I had to say that." His face breaks into a smile. "My guess is nothing will happen."

Nothing except Lucky is let out!

Lucky hangs around in the courthouse with Earl and lawyer Murphy and my father for the longest time. He looks bigger, like he's been working out, and his hair has grown out and he now has the shortest black buzz cut. He finally comes over to me, and I hand him the earring he gave me the day the police took him away, and he puts it right back on. I don't know if he's been changed by jail, and I don't know how much he blames me for his being sent there. He chats with me all naturally, like we're friends, but he doesn't touch me.

Chapter 32

Lucky is standing around, joking with some kids in front of the school when Freeland comes around the corner.

"Hey, Mr. Freeland. Look, Lucky's back. They let him out of the detention center."

Freeland's squinting like the sunlight is trapped inside his glasses. He grumbles hello.

"And a good morning to you, Principal Freeland!"

Freeland freezes.

"Anyway," Lucky goes on in his chipper voice, "I'm back."

Freeland ignores him and walks by.

"How's that search for the asbestos coming?"

Then another kid yells at Freeland's back. "Yeah, how about that asbestos?"

"Hold on," Lucky says. "Frank, cut it out."

"You are amazing," I say when the other kids are gone. "You could start a revolution."

He shrugs. "The cops are on my side on this one. The cops and you."

"Lucky, I never know what you're thinking about me. Am I like, this stupid bitch that got you in so much trouble? Is that why you won't talk to me now?"

"All I thought about in jail was that last day, on the sofa in your house."

"That time, it was like a dream. We were losing everything,

but it didn't matter."

"Yeah," he says, very low, "it was great." But he doesn't kiss me now, doesn't touch me now that he can. I can't stand it.

"Um, Lucky, this might sound really dumb, but I really don't know what you think about me. It seems like we're friends, and I want to know, like, are we?"

"Sure."

"I mean am I like your best friend?" Desperation has turned me into a complete dork. And right away I'm scared, thinking, if he says no, what am I going to do then – ask if I'm his second-best friend?

I could stand living with my mother if I could talk to Lucky every day. The old witch is now putting on a show, pretending to be like a real mother. Her lawyer is probably making her do it, and it's making everything worse. Now, she's actually there when I get home from school, and she stays there almost every minute. She's obviously bored to death, and so am I.

"You're really happier now that Lucky's back, aren't you?"

"Gee, Mom, you're so observant."

"How long is this sarcasm going to go on, Kate?"

"How long can you stand me being here all the time and you not being able to sleep with Anton? Or do you fuck him on the desk at the office?"

She wants to slap me, but then her famous control takes over.

"Don't do this, Kate. I don't deserve it."

"Mom, you practically told the judge I was fucking Dad."

"I didn't tell any lies. It was up to the judge to decide what it all meant."

"I'm not stupid, Mom. I'm not as pretty or smart as you, but I'm not deaf. I heard what you said about me. Why do you hate me? That's what I want to know."

Mr. Folsom looks even worse. He's been calling Dad, asking him in a real nervous way what his deposition was like. Even his new hairdo is getting greasy. Today he's wearing wrinkled pants and a thin green tie and looks like he's been sleeping on somebody's sofa. Near the end of class he puts an equation on the board and just keeps staring at it and mumbling. Then he drops his chalk and turns around.

"Those of you who have Ms. Nesbitt for English class will have a substitute teacher today. Ms. Nesbitt has been suspended.

"I was not even supposed to tell you that. Yes, she was suspended because of that outdoor class. That Transmutation class, where she showed you all that Principal Freeland was lying about the asbestos just to scare everybody."

"That sucks."

"Life isn't fair. You heard it here first." He never gets it together after that, and everybody just starts jabbering and Johnny Gott starts making fart noises.

I wait until everyone else is gone. Mr. Folsom is hunched over his desk with his face lost behind his black-framed glasses.

"I thought you were going to help us," I say.

"I tried."

He reaches into the top drawer of his desk and pulls out a piece of paper.

"It's a court order. I have to answer all of that bitch lawyer Mindy Faye's questions tomorrow or I'll be fined $500 a day until I do."

"Answer my questions first." I put my hand on his arm. "Tell me. What really happened that night in the woods?"

He stared at me, but I stared back until he saw I wasn't leaving until I got an answer. "Okay. I lost track of Randy that afternoon after school. Then I got a call from his after-school program that he hadn't shown up. I figured he was lost, and it was my fault, and I'd better find him on my own. And it really was my fault he was out there. I should have watched him more closely. It was my fault he was killed."

"Did you see him get shot?"

"I didn't see him at all. It was really dark out there! I thought they were shooting at me."

"Whoever shot him," I say. "That's whose fault it is. The one who pulled the trigger is the only one at fault. Right?" I'm telling this to myself too. Whoever shot him, and nobody else.

"It makes no difference to Mindy Faye. I'm a closet gay teacher. I was alone in the dark on the same trail as him on the night he got killed. I didn't tell anyone where I was going. I had no official reason to be there. I'll be fired, and then I'll be sued for everything I own. Then I'll probably be lynched."

The next day, Mr. Folsom freaks out again and lets us all wander out. Diane's fair skin is paler against her dyed purple hair. She holds her head high as always, but her eyes don't have their usual devilish look. She wants to go to the woods.

Ever since the murder there's been such parent panic that the teachers watch the halls like security guards, but today they pay no attention when we stroll out at ten in the morning. We lean into a cool wind all the way. It hasn't rained in so long that the leaves skitter into crunchy piles on the path. The early sun glares through the bare black tree limbs. Diane wears a blue leather coat, a nice contrast to her purple hair, which is now showing half an inch of light brown roots. We go down the path in the thin white sunlight and make our way to the drinking place. It's now carpeted with the gold leaves from the skeletal saplings. Diane suddenly gets down on her hands and knees and asks me to hold her hair while she throws up.

"So," I say, "you're still ...?"

"Yes."

"Are you feeling awful?"

"No. Usually just once a day I throw up. Really, Kate, it's not nearly as bad as the dry heaves."

We lie down next to each other in the leaves.

"How did it happen? I mean ..."

"I don't know. He said he was using a condom like you're supposed to."

"Does Carl know about it?"

"Know about it? Oh, yeah. He's so proud."

"What? What's that smile on your face?"

"I know it happens like a million times a week; but Kate, it's *real*, a real person is growing right inside *me*!"

I know I'm not as good a person as she is because all I'm thinking is how she's going out so far ahead of me and we'll never be in the same place again and I'll lose my best friend. Her hair is fanned out and shimmering in the grass, and I reach over and touch it, touch a real woman's hair.

"Carl wants me to marry him."

"Are you going to?"

"For God's sake, Kate, I'm not even fifteen."

"Where would you live?"

"He wants us to run away to Florida. I'm of legal age there, if I'm pregnant. He says we can live with his father until we find a place."

"Doesn't his father just rent a room?"

"Exactamento."

"Do you want to do that?"

"I don't know. I love him. That part is real. And a baby, that is real, believe me."

"But?"

She clenches her hands.

"I don't know, Kate. Now I really need him. But I would miss my friends! What would I do – be a teenage mother living four in a room in Florida, going out at night to get her GED?" She pounds her fists into the leaves. "Duh. Duh. Duh. Duh. Does this make sense?"

That night I dream that Mr. Folsom is back to his old self, glowing with joy over algebra. He's writing an equation on the board, but instead of exponents he's putting little white moons just above and to the right of the x's and y's. The first a quarter moon, the next a half moon, and so on. Somehow, it all makes perfect sense. In fact, it's more perfect than it ever actually has been with Mr. Folsom in real life. The equations fit together perfectly. Fit life perfectly. The moons are solid and brighter than anything else on the blackboard and they seemed to glow with the deepest truths of algebra. Somehow they get mixed up with Mr. Folsom's moon-eyes. I feel myself slipping into that ultra-calm state where algebra is coming from your own mind instead of being pounded into you. The connection between algebra and the moons and Mr. Folsom makes a perfect triangle, and I am inside and outside of the triangle at the same time. A dead quiet sweeps over the class, and we all instantly know all we really need to know.

I wake up right then, but it's still dark. I try to go back to sleep and go on with the dream, but it doesn't work. I notice that the window is lighter, so I push out from under my covers and crawl across the rug to the window to see if there is a moon outside. The air is clear and the stars are extra bright, more of them than I've ever seen before, a giant rhinestone belt across the middle of the sky. I've never seen the Milky Way before. I wish there was someone here to watch it with me.

I crawl back to the bed and lie there half asleep and thinking. I wonder what kind of mother Diane will be, if she's going to be a mother. I wonder if my mother really is innocent of the plot to put Lucky in jail over Alexander's Woods. Maybe she isn't that evil. Maybe there is a limit to how much she would hurt Lucky. But I doubt there's any limit to how much she would hurt me.

I called Dad earlier tonight. He egged me on to talk about Lucky. He loves hearing the happiness in my voice when I talk about him. He didn't ask anything about Mom. All I said to him was the witch was still alive.

Lucky won't go over to his father's house any more unless I'm with him, and I've been over there only once since Lucky got out. We knocked on the door, then poked our heads in and yelled until we were sure that Rudi wasn't there. Lucky's father pulled up in the driveway in a minute, and Lucky bounced over to meet him at the truck.

We sat at the kitchen table with Earl.

"At least the cops don't suspect either of us any more," Earl said. "Son, maybe it would've been better if we would of had a little faith in each other, told the cops all we knew right away."

"I knew it was our gun from the first."

"Well, we're both off the hook now anyway."

"Yeah. Great, Dad. Neither one of us is a murderer. How's that for a family recommendation, Kate?"

Earl stared at his hands. He and Lucky both stopped talking for a long time. They don't have to constantly talk like I always do with my friends. Then Earl stood up and jerked open the window like he was suffocating, then sat down again.

"I know," Earl turned to Lucky, his voice down low in his gravelly range, "if I got rid of Rudi, I'd have a better chance ... a better chance of getting you. But ..." Cool air filled the room from the open window. It was dark except for the pull-down lamp and the circle of light on the table. I was thinking – who's really in the circle, and who's out? "But I love that woman. She's not who I thought she was when I first chased after her. I used to call her the angel that chases the devil out of me." He took a long drink of his beer. "I don't know what the hell that means any more."

Earl spread his long fingers and slid them across the oilskin towards us. "I want her real bad, son. She's been real good for me. I know you've seen us argue a lot, but that's not what you think it is. I want her, and I want you, and I'll be damned if I won't get that working."

"Are you going to tell your father about Rudi?"

Lucky and I were in the bed of Earl's pickup truck. A bright slice of moon cut through the naked woods.

"I don't want anybody to know about that."

"Yeah, but doesn't it get to you when he goes on about how great she is?"

"Yeah."

"He won't get rid of her."

"He stopped drinking right after she moved in, but he's doing it again now. That means they're not getting along. Every time I see her she looks really bad. Maybe she'll leave on her own."

That night Lucky walked me up the steps to the outside door of Mom's apartment and we stood close. They say don't hang with kids who have obvious problems, but you don't really get to pick. I put my arms out for him blindly. I knew if he didn't step into my arms, I'd lose my balance and fall off the edge of the earth. When he caught me and held me tight, I was shaking.

"Are you crying?"

"No. No. No." I was laughing.

His kiss is all I can think about as I lie in my bed in Mom's apartment. I can't sleep. I want him here in bed with me right now. One thing I've learned since Mom first left was that wishing for things doesn't help at all. I am truly alone in my bedroom in my mother's apartment – which, it turns out, really is a model apartment that she got through her real estate friends. That is why it is furnished in that bland nursing-home way, and why she has only a three-month lease.

It's like living in a hotel where I can't get anything dirty. I take out a phone that I've been hiding and I punch in Diane's number. She has her own secret phone that Carl pays for that she keeps under her pillow. It's three o'clock in the morning, so I promise myself that I'll hang up if she doesn't answer the first ring; but I break my promise. Ten long rings. She must be sound asleep, or not there. I hang up.

The bedroom is so quiet now. It seems even more hollow and artificial at night. My days here with Mom are so dry. Only a couple of weeks ago I was free in the woods, skating with Lucky – or kissing him in the parking lot under the moon while we leaned with weak knees against his father's pickup truck. I remember looking up at that moon and thinking I could never be unhappy again.

I didn't know then all the things that could happen, all the ways that people could be different from what you thought. Now I'm forced to live with the witch in this dry apartment like a rat in a cage. My living here is putting such a crimp in her love life that she's getting super bitchy, just like she did before she left home. I don't belong here. Why do I have to live this artificial life in the control of the witch? Living here while Dad needs me at home is just wrong. And the next thing I'm afraid of is maybe Dad will get used to being alone. Then if I ever do come home it will be too late and I won't belong anywhere, and I'll grow up an old, twisted mini-witch myself.

I can feel Lucky around me everywhere: when I'm lying in this bed, when I'm getting up, when I'm being driven to school, whenever I'm doing my homework and bored out of my mind but hearing him say "just do it and get it over with." When we meet at school, there is never a second of awkwardness. Lucky can't stand living at his mother's either. His mother and Ralph are arguing a lot. Ralph is always complaining about having to stay home alone to watch Lucky.

The thought of him is not enough right now. I miss him so much I can't lie still. I sit up in bed, trying to think of something else. I crawl over to the window again and put my hands against the glass and look up into the sky. There's something comforting in all the stars being so big and so far away, with maybe millions of other worlds floating around them too, with billions of people who have problems bigger than mine.

The worst thing that happened to Johnson was not that he died, but that he had to live the way he did. He was trapped so much worse than Lucky and I ever were. And while Lucky and I are mad about who we have to live with, Johnson was not allowed to live at all. He was forced into somebody else's crazy idea of a life. Mr. Folsom says it does matter who killed him. Why can't they find out who did it? Principal Freeland sent Lucky to jail for doing nothing, so I don't see why Freeland wouldn't do a murder too. Maybe it was his and Anton's way of telling everybody to keep away from the woods.

Maybe ...

I wake up for a minute with my cheek numb from being pressed into my hands. Then I fall asleep and dream that Freeland is chasing me through the woods in the dark, but I have a skateboard and he can't catch me. I keep skating down and down the path into the darkness, but I don't know any more where the path goes. I wake again and look at the sky. The stars are disappearing and a veil of thin grey clouds begins dimming them as I fall asleep again. I dream about Mr. Folsom. He's at the blackboard, and this time there are little glowing stars as well as moons as the exponents of his equations. In this dream I remember the first dream. I want to believe again that the glowing exponents can give us the answers and explain everything, but this time I don't really believe it's true. And then I see what's wrong. The triangle is missing. That was the connection in the first dream – between me and Mr. Folsom and those starry and moony exponents. I'm afraid that I've been excluded from the triangle and that I'll be locked outside forever. But then I notice that the exponents are still glowing, and that I still know them well, and that it is Mr. Folsom who is outside of the triangle. I try to bring him in, but the closer I come, the fainter he gets, until he totally disappears. When I wake up again the stars are gone and the sky is completely blackened over with clouds.

233

Chapter 33

Lucky is pacing the sidewalk in front of school, looking in the windows of every car that stops because he doesn't know my mother's car.

"What's the matter?"

"Come around back." He stares the other kids off until we are alone behind the blank brick wall of the school.

"What?"

"Mr. Folsom."

"What about him?"

"He slit his wrists last night."

"No!"

"He didn't die, but he's in the hospital. Walton, that cop, told me they are going to put him in the psychiatric ward after they sew him up. He'll never be back."

"I was just talking to him yesterday."

"He was the best one. He was the best teacher."

"He was so afraid."

"You talked to him a lot. What was he so afraid of?"

"Of what people would think."

All they say over the PA system in school is we will have a substitute teacher. When the substitute doesn't show, Lucky stands up in front of the class.

"They won't tell us the truth, so here's what really happened."

Mom's apartment is so quiet I feel like I have to scream. The algebra book is sitting where I last threw it on my bedroom floor. The thing about Mr. Folsom was he made me believe there is a reason for all of the crap we have to put up with in junior high school. I guess he didn't have a reason of his own.

Mom is okay with me not eating my dinner. I go into my room and close the door to do my homework. I can't look at the algebra book, can't pick it up, can't even kick it out of the way. I try to call Diane but she's not home. Neither is Lucky. I open my English book and start a project Ms. Nesbitt assigned before she got suspended.

Dad calls. Before I can tell him anything he says, "I know. I know."

"Kate, you received a letter here today, from Mr. Folsom."

Chapter 34

She still loved me. I was sure of it, despite the fact that she wouldn't look at me when we left the courtroom. Since then I had talked to her on the phone every day. Clare hated this, but she knew she had to let Kate call me.

One afternoon after work, I decided to walk down the trail to that bridge where everyone said the Johnson boy was shot. The first heavy frost of the year had finally silenced the last of the crickets. The only sound at the trail level was the rasp of the dry weeds rattling against my jeans. The wind made a constant dull roar high in the trees.

The horizon was a thicket of bare branches seventy feet in the air. Above them, soft blobs of grey clouds floated across. Dark pines and cedars stood alone; all the rest was a chaotic lushness of fallen vines and drooping branches and spent purple brush. The sunlight was bright but very thin. Everything in those woods was slowly and beautifully dying.

At the bridge, near the murder site, the stream gurgled cheerily enough below. There weren't many rocks in the stream there, and the water ran clear over a sandy bed flecked with sparkles of mica. I walked out to the middle of the bridge, enjoying the hollow sound my hiking boots made on the boards.

It was moonlit there the night Johnson died. Things always seem the most beautiful just as you are losing them. There will never be clearer air, or a more intensely green field, or a bluer sky, or more piercing crimson and white flowers, than those I saw that April day when I buried my mother. This was a day made for a loss like that.

As the path curved away from the stream, a graveyard of fallen trees, their huge trunks smooth and bleached and bare, lay together in a clearing. I lay down on top of the biggest one. I could hear the stream each time the wind paused for breath. A woodpecker rapped like a machine gun not far off. There were a few crows circling just above the tallest trees. I could hear a squirrel under the brush, frantically gathering the last of the nuts. No one ever contemplated life and death in a place more beautiful than this.

I sank deeper and deeper into the past. My mother came to me. She was with me somewhere under the wind, listening to all the sounds of the woods with me. I should have buried her here, on her own land. If her body were here, her spirit would not be so restless and would not haunt me so much. My soul still craved her. I knew that was not right, unless it was my turn to die.

I could only worship women. Meeting them halfway always seemed like too cold a business. The kind of love I craved grew out of the past, but in the present it was never quite there but always just around the corner. When it seemed real, for a few short years, it turned out to be real only for me, a fire inside without any fuel. It was a sickness. I was a worshipper of sickness. I cried as I let my mother caress me one last time. There would never be anyone else who really understood the soaring gravity of this place.

Chapter 35

Triandos called it work therapy. I kept busy at the office, slapping down doubts and jumping on projects and injecting coffee instead of those meals that still would not go down. I realized that for many years I had done no more work than the minimum needed to make sure that Triandos still liked me.

"I'm going all out to get Kate back," I told to him the day after I lost the temporary custody hearing. "I'm tired of being screwed by her bastard lawyer."

"You know, Sam, the lawyers just do what their clients ask them to do. Clare's the one who really grabbed you by the short hairs."

"Oh, Triandos, you're full of it." I turned back toward my office, knowing that he was exactly right, and knowing that he knew I knew that he was exactly right.

One morning he waved me into his office. "Sam, sometimes the government process stinks so much I'm ashamed to be a part of it. I have friends in the County Attorney's office. There's a bill being secretly drafted right now. It only applies to your part of the county. It gives the County Executive special temporary powers to condemn land and rezone it for economic development purposes."

"The County Executive is directly involved in this?"

Triandos shrugged. "If it passes, the county can take your property by condemnation and sell it back to a developer. Any guesses as to who that developer might be?"

"You wouldn't, by any chance, have a copy of this secret bill, right in your pocket right now, would you?"

"Take a look." Triandos was excited. He handed it to me but couldn't wait for me to actually read it. "It really only applies to the grounds of Glenwood Junior High School and to Alexander's Woods. It basically gives the County Executive the power to take the woods away from you and give them to Anton."

"They must be pretty sure of themselves to be that blatant."

"You better make sure the bill doesn't pass."

"And I do that – how? Tell everybody that it's just a get-rich-quick scheme with a cut for county politicians?"

"That's what every zoning bill is."

Over the next few days, Triandos and I eagerly read the newspapers, listened to the radio and spent time speculating about what might happen next. I made all the calls I could to all the politicians who ever represented me. I got only one on the line, and the best I could get was a vague promise to look into it. My regular workload was also heavy, but I did that too because I owed Triandos a lot and wanted him to be proud of me. As a result, a couple of full workdays went by without memories of Clare sucking at my soul. I answered the phone when it rang without first praying that it would be her. I got through a few days that way, and I thought I could do a few more.

Chapter 36

Before I read Mr. Folsom's letter I want to be smart enough to understand it. I know he said he didn't do it, but I'm still afraid the letter might be a confession. The worst thing I can imagine is him saying he did it for me.

Mom's getting restless in the evenings, just like she used to when she had to stay home with Dad. She changes her earrings twice after dinner.

"Every minute you're with me, you think you're wasting your time, don't you?"

"That's not true, Kate, but ..."

"There's always a 'but,' isn't there, Mom?"

"No, but ..."

"See! 'But' again."

Her lips close in a tight line.

"I admit it's frustrating to me. You lie around all afternoon looking out the window. You're always on the phone with Diane or Lucky. I ask you a question and you look at me like I have some contagious disease. So you're right, I don't enjoy it. I keep thinking, if you'd get your work done in an efficient manner, we'd have time to do all kinds of things, worthwhile things, get to know each other again."

"So, if I was a more efficient person, you'd like me."

"That's not what I said. Oh, Kate, do you have to punish me and punish me and punish me, all because I fell out of love with your father?"

I hear her later talking to Anton on the phone in her room. She does this all the time, and thank God I usually can't hear it. When she's on the phone with Anton, her voice is deep and full, and she'll burst into giggles like she's getting little sexual shocks over the line. But it's a different tone tonight, a lower, secret voice that tempts me to listen in on the extension in the living room.

"Backfired?" she's saying. "You might say that. There's a rumor that the FBI might investigate Freeland for pressuring the police to put that poor boy in jail. He comes off looking like Darth Vader in the newspaper. And you don't look much better."

"Yeah, Clare. Well, shit happens. We'll be okay, babe. But Clare?"

"Yes?"

"We have to fight back. It might be time to put the real screws to Sam."

"What do you mean?"

"The things Sam told you. His sicko feelings. Threaten to publish the transcript in the press."

"I don't know."

"Babe, have I been wrong yet?"

"You've taught me so much."

"Do it. Tell him the transcript will be distributed everywhere. Like to his boss. He works for the county, right? They can fire you for domestic abuse."

"What good would that do us?"

"Our zoning bill was sailing through the county council until this story about Freeland and the juvenile got out. We can't get that land from the county now, babe. We got to go and squeeze it right out of Sam now."

"So we threaten to publish his own testimony, so everybody will think he's a pervert?"

"Yeah, babe."

"God, Mom, you both sound so dumb! Anton's just rich. He's not smart."

Anton bursts in the door.

"It's over! It's over!"

But he stops when he sees me.

"You ought to teach your daughter some manners."

I walk away.

"She's a kid, Anton. She's upset."

"So am I. We're screwed, Clare. It's over. I just talked to the County Executive. He didn't just drop the special zoning bill. He told me he'd deny me building permits even if I got the land on my own. I offered him a bigger piece of the company. He said all he wanted from me was deniability."

"Oh honey. Oh honey, it's just one project." Mom is laying on the love.

"You have anything to drink?"

The refrigerator door opens and closes.

"Don't do that." It's Anton's voice, low. "Not now. I'm not in the mood."

"I can cure that mood."

"No, you can't."

Chapter 37

The special zoning bill allowing Anton to take my property, which had previously been zipping through the county council approval process with record speed, suddenly died. Word of Freeland's dirty tricks with Lucky, and Freeland's connections to the County Executive, had been leaked to the press.

I called Kate.

"The stories in the paper are blowing up Anton's scheme."

"I already heard it from the whore's mouth."

"Stop it, Kate. She's still your mother. But how did the paper find out that Freeland put Lucky in jail over this?"

"Maybe it was that cop Walton. He and Lucky are really tight."

"Kate, I told you the principal can't have somebody put in jail just on his say-so. I knew that wouldn't happen."

"Are you blind or something, Dad? He did it. He put Lucky in jail. Lucky only got out because the police lost the evidence. He put Lucky in jail, Dad. He has to be put in jail himself now."

"I don't think that's going to happen, Kate."

There was a little danger point at work every weekday morning, right after the time we spent on this delicious county gossip and just before we actually started on our work. If I didn't dive right into my work right away, Clare's spirit would sit on my shoulder and whisper into my brain. Nothing could stop the voice, but picking up the phone and arguing with someone about business helped a little.

But that day I followed Triandos instead, walking right behind him into his office and sitting down, facing him.

"I need to thank you."

"Oh. Well. It's okay. Don't worry about it."

"I mean, just because I don't say anything, doesn't mean that I haven't noticed how you backed me up, how good you've been to me through all of this."

His dark eyes watched me. Then he just shrugged.

"I never had a father," I said. "I didn't know what they were for. Your sons are so lucky."

Chapter 38

We have a new principal at school. Lucky's father's contract to tear down the soccer stands is cancelled, and his new job is to tear down the chain link fences Freeland put around the school property. The papers can't use Lucky's name, but everybody knows that Lucky is the kid who was put away because of Freeland's blackmail. One night I hear the witch answer the door, and I hear Anton's voice. They go into her room and close the door, but he leaves an hour later.

At breakfast the next morning, I can tell her whole body is tense.

"So, Mom, Anton's not going to get rich off of Alexander's Woods after all."

"I don't know if he's rich, honey. I never asked him if he was rich or not."

"He should be in jail. Freeland should be too."

"Kate, I want you to listen to me. Anton did nothing wrong. There are always obstacles in the way of development; there are always people who are unhappy with it. You do have to push your way around if you want to get anything done. But if I thought for a minute that he was involved in what Mr. Freeland did to Lucky, that would be the end. Period."

"Lucky found out the police had orders to pick him up whenever Freeland told them to."

"Anton didn't know anything about it, Kate. Freeland and

the County Executive must have done it on their own."

"But Freeland was doing that for Anton. You keep forgetting, Mom – he told me."

"Believe what you want, Kate." She pulls things out of the cabinet and slams them down on the counter.

"But what you did to me, Mom, was worse."

She folds a stiff brown paper bag like it's a weapon of war. "I just went by what he, your father, told me," she screams, "and by what you told me!"

"You wanted to believe that I am a slut. You wanted to believe it because you hate me, and I'll never figure out why."

I get to my room but don't get the door shut in time. She stands over me, and she's not angry any more.

"Kate, maybe we should face it. This isn't working."

She looks relieved now, like she's found out what was the trouble. She's just catching on to what I've known for years.

"You really don't like me, right?"

"I don't hate you, Kate. But everything that I've ever tried to do for you – it seems like you spoil it on purpose."

"How?"

"I don't know. But it seems like you spoiled everything on purpose ... like you didn't want to be my daughter."

"I did."

"But it didn't seem like that to me. It didn't seem like you were really my daughter."

I used to think the screaming and accusing was as bad as it could get.

She sits down on the edge of the bed. "So, what I was thinking ... we just don't get along. Maybe you'd be better off living with your father."

"You said he was abusing me."

"I'm not worried about that any more. Things change."

"What's changed?"

She stands up like she doesn't have to answer me. She takes

246

a deep breath, looking past me at the wall, then walks out of the room.

"Dad," I'm crying on the phone. Lucky is holding my hand. "Do you want me back?"

"I don't think that can happen, Kate."

"She's kicking me out, Dad. I don't know what's wrong with me. If you want me back, come pick me up *right now*!"

I hang up and turn to Lucky.

"Lucky, on the trail that night, you said to keep my head down, but I looked up anyway. I saw who ran up the trail. It was Folsom. I'm sorry I didn't tell you."

He nods. "I saw him too. I'm never telling anybody."

"Why did we lie to each other?" He just stares back. "There's something else I need to tell you. I got a letter from him."

Dear Kate,

You are the only person I know who I think deserves a goodbye. You are a talented student and you have the heart to be a good woman.

It's too painful to go on, and so I'm ending it. It hurts me to know that you believed in me when I was a fraud. The truth is I've never been any good for anyone. I would like to believe that everybody has a chance. If I ever had one, I must have missed out on it somewhere. I think you have a chance to do better than me.

All I tried to do was protect you and the other kids from Johnson, and protect him too as much as I could. All the decisions about where he went to school and what class he was in and what he was supposed to learn and who was his aide were made by somebody else, but nobody was held responsible for what happened but me. They were going to torture me for it. I'm sure you can see that.

Just to be sure, since this is my last human

communication – I did not kill Randy Johnson, and I did not see anybody at all in the woods that night.

You and your father are decent people, some of the very few who have been kind to me. I wish I could say that about the rest of the school. I have no doubt you'll make it to the moon, Kate, whatever your particular moon might be. And when you do, give it a kick in the pants in memory of me.

Goodbye,
John Folsom

I hand the letter to Lucky. He reads it, then sags back onto the sofa.

I hug Dad as hard as I can, and I won't let go.

"Are you making a statement, Kate?"

I'm laughing and crying.

"I missed you too, Kate. If you can forgive me for all the stupid things I did in the last few weeks, we will be all right."

I read him the letter from Mr. Folsom.

"I knew him, Dad. I really knew him. He must have been just pretending to like me all the time."

"Pretending?"

"I mean, it didn't do him any good."

"You don't know that, Kate. Maybe he thought about you at the last minute. Maybe that's why he called 911. You give yourself to somebody, and you never know how it's going to turn out. But you have to keep doing it."

We read the letter one more time, then decide to burn it.

"She really, really doesn't want me, Dad."

"Even after all this, it could turn out all right in the end."

"It won't. I absolutely know that."

Chapter 39

Corporal Walton is with Lucky at the head of the trail one morning. Now that Lucky has a little hair, Walton looks like the radical one.

"He wants to take us to the station and show us something."

"What?"

"We're not under arrest or anything, right?" Lucky looks at Walton. "But we still have to go?"

"You want to go."

He takes us into a little room, sits us down, and closes the door.

"You know he was shot with your father's gun, right?"

Lucky nods.

"Of course it wasn't either you or your father. We have fingerprints on the gun from the person who did it."

"So, you brought us here to tell us who?"

Corporal Walton has a weird smile on his face.

"Yeah, I'm going to tell you." But he doesn't.

"What? Are we supposed to guess?" Lucky is freaked out that Walton is being so cagey. "It was Rat, right? He found that gun somehow."

"Not Rat. He wasn't there." Walton's smile disappears, and he stares at me. "Any other suspects, Kate? Anyone else who could have been on the trail that night? Anyone you may have forgotten to mention?"

I can feel my face turn red. He knows I lied to him, and he waits so I can feel ashamed. I know what I saw that night, but I still believe Mr. Folsom.

"It wasn't Folsom." Corporal Walton's eyes are waiting to meet mine when I look up. "It wasn't Folsom. But we did waste a lot of time trying to identify the person who ran out of the woods. A lot of time while the real killer could have gotten away, or murdered somebody else."

He looks at me so long that I know this is why he brought us here.

"I didn't care who killed him. I never thought about ... what you just said."

"You *should* think about that. You're only fourteen, but in the future you should think about things like that."

"So," Lucky says, "did the real killer get away?"

"No. The fingerprints on that gun belonged to Randy Johnson. We found his fingerprints on the gun, and we also found them on the steel pole that holds up your father's birdhouse."

"Oh."

"Oh my God!" Lucky says.

Of course, nobody told Johnson where that gun was. He must have been close behind me that night. He must have come in the yard after I was gone and popped open the roof of that birdhouse just like I was trying to do when Duke and Molson knocked me down. So the gun was there and it was loaded when I reached for it. And so Johnson was right behind me. And when I remember how scared I was, and what I might have done, I'm so grateful for those dogs, those wonderful dogs. But then it hits me how awful Johnson must have felt to do that to himself.

"He said he loved me that day."

Lucky and Corporal Walton both look at me.

"It was right after he was jacking off on the bridge. I was so scared. And I was awful to him, really awful to him. I knew he would never keep away from me unless I really hurt him. And that's what I did."

Lucky looks at Walton.

"Johnson definitely did it himself." Lucky says, and he and Walton nod together, as if all that matters is who actually pulled the trigger. But I know now there are other ways of killing.

"Normally, we'd just close an investigation like this quietly. Tell the family without any announcement. But there's going to be a press conference right at the school on this one. Chief insisted on this. He hit the ceiling when Randy's mother sued him for not solving this crime."

"A press conference?"

"To close the case. I wouldn't advise you to go. It's going to be nasty. I'll tell you two the truth. It wasn't even a clean suicide. It's ... it's just the ugliest thing I've ever seen."

They bring back Ms. Nesbitt the minute Freeland resigns. It doesn't take long for her to get back to what is normal – for her.

"Put your coats on," she commands. "We're going to have one of our outdoor classes."

"We know for sure now that the woods are safe." Ms. Nesbitt lectures us as we walk down the path into the woods. There is no sound but the crunching of leaves under twenty pairs of feet. No one complains about the cold. A couple of crows flying high above are the only signs of animal life.

"Stop for a minute. Listen to the sound of the wind pushing its way through the forest."

Then we walk on. Around the next bend we see a group of guys hanging out on the trail, smoking cigarettes and passing around a whiskey bottle. When they see this is a class, with a teacher, they pass the bottle to the two guys behind, but those two guys keep swigging on the bottle. One of them is Rat.

"Hey, it's Lucky the snitch!" Rat calls out. Ms. Nesbitt stops, and so do we. Lucky doesn't say anything.

"Lucky, can't you hear me?" Rat is yelling and also waving the whiskey bottle in the air. Lucky walks real slowly down ahead of us until he is standing right in front of Rat. Rat's group opens up, and they all mill around. Lucky has his hands in his pockets. His hair is almost as long now as Rat's buzz cut. I'm watching to see if Rat reaches for the knife he carries on his belt, but they're all laughing. Lucky waves us forward.

"Morning, Ms. Nesbitt," Rat calls out.

She stares at him. "Ellwood? Is that you? Oh yes, good morning to you. I didn't know what you'd been doing since you dropped out. Now I know where I can find you."

"Ellwood? His name is Ell-wood?" Diane drags out the word.

"Hey, Kate! How ya been? Last time I seen you, you were kneeling next to that stump over there puking out your guts."

This gets a big laugh. My face is hot. There's nothing I can do but give him a little wave and march on by.

We come to the bridge. Some of the guys are looking for bloodstains, and they're not hard to find. Ms. Nesbitt walks out to the middle of the bridge and stands there looking back at us. She bows her head until everyone's quiet.

"There's a lesson here," she says quietly. "Everyone says these woods are dangerous. In a way, they are. Once in a hundred years one of these giant oak trees falls and kills somebody. But that didn't happen today, and it's not likely to ever happen to any of us.

"There are dangerous animals in the woods. But mostly the wild animals go out of their way to keep away from us.

"Much more dangerous are the people you might meet in the woods. We saw some people today, wild drunken people who have been known to shoot off guns. You could get hurt by a person like that; but again, it's not really very likely.

"Randy Johnson wasn't hurt by any of these things. On this

bridge, Randy Johnson ran into the most dangerous opponent of all – himself. He couldn't conquer that opponent, and he died.

"You all have to realize that you yourself are your most dangerous opponent. Recognize that. Look inside yourself. That's where you will find the hard things you have to face. That's where you will find your own personal demons. That's where you will find what's holding you back and what's making you afraid. Don't be looking in the woods for something to be afraid of."

Diane pulls me aside. Her eyes are red.

"Carl left for Florida."

"What did he say?"

"He said he loves me too much. He said he couldn't stand to hang around me the rest of his life, loving me so much, unless I'll be his wife. He left this morning. I know he's kind of dumb, Kate, but I really love him."

"You were already fighting, even before you got pregnant."

"I know, but I miss him. I'm crying all the time. We made this baby, and it's the best thing I've ever done in my whole life, and I know it's the best thing he's ever done. I should marry him. I'm really craving to be with him all the time, but – I don't know. I just can't."

"Who wants to live four in a rented room in Florida?"

"I know. But I guess it wouldn't always be that way. He can make money. I could too somehow. It would be a real life. It's something I never had."

"What do you mean?"

"Kate, it's real with Carl. I can feel it. I'm giving him up, and I know I'll never have another chance."

"Everybody loves you, Diane."

"You think so? It doesn't seem like it."

"It's true."

"That's just because I'm usually a half step ahead of them.

Now that I've done the most uncool thing ever, everybody will shit all over me."

"No, they won't. And you're still the best."

"I wish everybody was like you, Kate." We're back up the trail, almost to the school. She's been crying, but as we get closer to the school she sniffs a few last times and holds her head high.

"What it is, Kate – there's something so stupid about his whole plan. I just can't get with the idea of being fifteen years old, holding our baby, sitting around watching him wash his car all day."

It's creepy to realize the police or the morgue or somebody has been keeping Johnson's body frozen all this time, but it's true, and there's going to be a funeral.

"I'm going."

"Are you crazy?" Lucky says. "It's finally over. Let it go."

"It's not over. Something's not over."

Lucky goes with me to the funeral home, a one-story brick building in the same industrial park where Lucky goes to have his urine tested. A short, white-haired man in a mustard-colored suit comes up to us inside the door and shows us what room to go to. He leads us down a floral-carpeted hallway and helps us sneak into the back of the room where Johnson is laid out. No one else from school is here. Johnson's mother is up front where the coffin is.

We're too late to hear anything but a snatch of the minister's speech: God loved Randy so much he made him special, blah, blah.

Johnson is lying in a metal coffin with his face all made up.

"He does look like he's at peace."

"He looks like a wax sculpture."

We get in line with a bunch of people who are taking one last look at Randy. Up close, the sight of that face makes me shake.

Lucky holds me.

"This is scary."

"Then why did we come?"

"I don't know. To make sure he really is dead?"

"He is. We should go now."

We are leaving and almost at the door when the man in the mustard suit stops us.

"Mrs. Johnson would like you to travel to the graveyard in the limousine with her."

We didn't know it would be just Mrs. Johnson, her sister, and the two of us. I guess Mrs. Johnson doesn't have a husband, or any other children.

"It was very nice of you to come," the sister says. "It's nice to meet some of Randy's friends."

"Yeah," Lucky says.

"That school," Johnson's mother begins, "They put so much pressure on him. And I know all the kids teased him. He just couldn't take it."

"He shouldn't have been in a regular class." My words sink into the soft cloth walls of the limousine.

"He had a right ..." Her voice trails off again. Our car pulls in behind the limousine with the coffin in it.

"He shouldn't have been in any class where there were girls." I can't stop myself.

She gives me an evil stare with tight lips. She is never going to accept that whenever I even looked at Randy, he tried to hurt me. She will never change her mind. So I can't stop attacking her.

"The school let him do whatever he wanted. He hurt me every time I tried to talk to him. You know why I think he killed himself? I think he did it because he just hated the way he was."

Her sister grabs her hand, and Lucky grabs my shoulder. He looks at me and shakes his head. Of course, he's right. I know I should shut up. Still, the whole thing makes me so mad I have to yell at somebody, or cry.

My tears are a little bit for Johnson too. He was so alone, and he did love me, and he thought I could save him. His love was dangerous, and it hurt me – but what is so different about that? I know now there's all kinds of love, and his love was one kind, and maybe not even the most painful kind.

It's been raining hard all morning, taking even more leaves off the trees; now it's slowed to a drizzle. There's so much mist near the ground it's like the grey sky has lowered itself down to the earth. We step out of the limo onto grass that's thick and green but squishy underneath.

They put the coffin on a kind of web that's suspended over the grave. I think about Johnson's body really being in there, and really being ready to be put down in that wet, cold hole. I feel sorry for anybody who has to die as a kid. Johnson didn't ask to be born with his brain all scrambled and crazy. It's hard to believe God did it out of love.

I wouldn't have hurt him so much if I hadn't been so scared. That's why I'm here. I'm here because I hurt him. But there's something else, something about the way I hurt him.

There's a bunch of folding wooden chairs set up in rows under a tarp to keep people out of the dripping rain. Most people are huddled together near the front. Lucky and I are standing right behind Johnson's mother and her sister. The mist blows cold at the back of our necks. All the other people there are old, old and huddled up toward the front.

The soft closing of a car door behind us makes me jump. I turn around and see Anton squishing through the grass towards us. Long black raincoat, no umbrella, no hat to cover his wig. Mom's car is up on the road behind him.

"Your mother," Anton practically shouts out to me, like there's nobody else here and nothing else going on, "would like to drive you and Lucky home afterwards."

He stands there, arms folded, through the rest of the service. Mindy Faye, the lawyer, also shows up, arriving really late and carrying a huge umbrella that doesn't quite fit under the tent and drips all over the people standing next to her. After all the praying is over, they don't even bury the coffin in the ground. They just leave it hanging over the grave. Lucky and I have to figure out for ourselves that it's over.

"We got two choices," Lucky whispers to me. "Your mother or Johnson's mother."

"I can't go back in that limousine."

"How was the funeral?"

Mom still has her real estate blazer on. Lucky and I are sitting together in the back. The windows steam up so much that she has to let the defroster run a minute before driving.

"You got to get a new car." Anton acts annoyed. "A little bigger – get a Mercedes this time."

"I just got this one paid off. Three years of $743 a month."

"Three years ago? Wasn't that about the time you started telling Dad we couldn't afford vacations?"

"It's so much fun," my mother rolls her eyes, "to see my whole life re-interpreted for me – with me as the Bitch Queen in every scene."

Anton turns around to face us. I'm only fourteen, and he's forty, but I already know that he is just a spoiled baby. His soaking wig is dripping onto his forehead.

"Why don't you cut your mother a break?"

"Are you giving her a Mercedes?"

"I'll give her whatever I want."

"I heard you're going broke." Lucky has decided to join the happy family conversation.

Anton's eyes switch over to Lucky.

"I heard you finally blew all the money your father left you," Lucky adds.

"You hear that, Mom? You might want to reconsider this romance. Get out while the getting's good."

"Stop the car. I'm going to clean his clock."

"I certainly am not. And you certainly are not going to touch that boy."

Anton turns back around. We drive for a while in silence as the rain pounds on the car. Anton pretends he's talking to my mother.

"All the little shits in Glenwood like his father hate me. They're jealous on account of my father."

"My father used to know your father," Lucky pipes in from the back seat. "You know what your father told my father one day? One time when he was drunk, he told my father he couldn't stand the sight of you."

"Rudi and I have been talking real serious. We have serious troubles."

Lucky and I have gone with Earl back to his house. When Earl snaps on the switch, the overhead light catches the look on both of our faces.

"Don't look so scared. I'm just trying to be straight with you."

"About what?" Lucky finds his voice first, weak as it is.

"It's bad. Rudi's leaving."

I don't dare look at Lucky.

"I already drove one good woman out of my life. I can't let it happen again. I'm not much of a man if I drive out all the women I love."

"There could be a lot of reasons for her leaving," I blurt out. Is this the worst possible thing to say or what? But I hate it that he thinks there's something wrong with him that's making her leave. That was what Dad thought when Mom left.

"They all do eventually turn against me. Lately I've been thinking maybe it's my own fault."

"It's not your fault. Everybody likes you, Dad."

"You like me, Lucky. Yeah, I guess some other people do too." Earl's permanent smile comes out even now. He is so much like his son. He and Lucky are so comfortable with each other it makes me jealous. But I know Lucky is scared.

Earl's eyes dart away.

"Lucky, go on out and take care of those dogs for a while. You know where the dog food is. I'm going to lay back in here and talk to Kate for a while."

Oh shit.

"And hey, Lucky, did you take that gun out again?"

"The police gave us back the gun?"

"You didn't take it out of the drawer?"

"Didn't know we had it back."

"Don't look so scared, Kate. I just want to ask you something, you know, from a woman's point of view."

"Oh."

"Your opinion."

"I'm not really a woman."

"Ha!"

I sit down at the table.

"What do you think I could do," he says, "to get Rudi to stay?"

"Did she say she's leaving?"

"She put all her stuff in the car."

"I'm sure it's not your fault." I've never been so sure of anything in my life. But then all of a sudden there's something else, something I'm not sure of.

"I said she could start a craft shop. I said we could get married. I'll do anything to keep that woman. She's good for me. Without her, I'm just another broke-down, drunken hillbilly."

Earl means what he says, but something else is bothering me and I stop listening to what he's saying. I'm back on the bridge with Randy Johnson the night he died. I'm talking to him and then watching his face crumple with a sadness like I've never seen before.

The noise of a car starting outside puts it all together. I run out past Earl, through the dogs, past Lucky and chase down that little brown car backing down the driveway and jump in the passenger door.

"Get out, honey. I'm giving you what you want."

"No." Earl and Lucky are running down the driveway after us. She floors it, and you can hear the gravel spitting out from underneath. She goes fast until we are around a curve, behind thick brush that hides us from the house. Then she slams on the brakes.

"Get out!"

I grab the steering wheel with both hands and fight with her.

"Give me the gun."

My hand is on her wrist, but she curls her fingers around the keys and pulls herself free. She bumps her face against the steering wheel and leaves it there, her eyes closed, her whole body curled up and shrinking away from me. I climb over and grab her and she screams and fights but ends up sobbing in my arms. I told Randy Johnson on the bridge that night that he was not human, that he was a monster. And when that didn't make him sad enough I told him that he should kill himself because everybody would be better off if he was dead.

"Let me die."

"You can start over someplace else. Nobody will ever tell Earl."

"I'm no good. Just let me die, honey. You know what I am."

"You are not." I slap her really hard. "You are not a hole."

Over the past few months I must have gone to the window

a thousand times, hoping to see Clare's blue Acura pulled up in front, each time dreaming of the flood of relief that miracle would bring. I'd been trying to teach myself that it would never happen.

And since I had taught myself so well, the flood of relief did not come on that Saturday when that car did pull up. Clare killed the engine and got out, but I no longer believed that anything good would come of it. My heart was cowering in my chest.

"I've come to bring the rest of Kate's things over."

"Okay."

"Will you help me unload them out of the car?"

"Sure."

We piled several boxes of stuff up next to the huge pile of clothing and junk that Kate had already re-established in her room. Clare turned around suddenly and sat on one of the boxes, facing me.

"I told my lawyer to drop the custody suit."

"Good."

"I'll call Social Services on Monday and tell them there is no need to do an abuse investigation. Okay?"

All I needed to do was to come up with one word of gratitude. But I couldn't do it. Some reflex told me I was going to be hurt again, and that reflex was stronger than common sense.

"I don't deserve to be thanked." She ran her hands down her thighs to her knees and hung her head down and looked at the floor.

"It's the right thing to do," was all I could manage.

"Have you made a lot of changes?" She stood and walked slowly up to me. I didn't know what she was doing, so I kind of backed into the hallway. Then she went right to the door of what used to be our bedroom and walked in. I had a sudden surge of panic.

"You haven't changed anything."

Okay, I kept telling myself that I was going to do it, change things around – at least move the few remaining pictures so they'd be centered right. But leaving these things just as she left them was still part of my sense of balance. Moving them would throw me off, and I hadn't been able to do that just yet. What she saw just then was very much like a museum of our love, mute proof that I was still in her power.

She took her time, walking around the bed (the same spread, the same blanket), looking at all the pictures and knickknacks. One thing that had changed was that now there was dust over everything. She sat down on the bed.

"I don't think Kate will ever forgive me."

My feet froze in place, and I had to lean against the wall.

"I haven't told her the half of what you did."

"That must have been hard. You're a good man, Sam." Clare held her arms close to her sides, her hands flat on the bed on each side. She looked around the room again, then caught my attention with her slow, green-eyed gaze. I put my hands back against the wall.

I steadied myself as the silence between us grew. She looked at me again with those beautiful eyes, eyes that were now glazed with tears. My soul had withered away for lack of this nourishment. I put out my arms and she ran into them. Both of us were sobbing.

Drinking in her touch, I couldn't focus. Her face was buried in my neck, but she didn't cry. And then I started to think. That's what you have to do sometimes.

"I love you, Clare. But it hurts too much. You hurt Kate too much. You have to leave."

Chapter 40

Dad drops me off in his minivan. There's a new principal, and now there's a new math teacher at school. They're okay. They're trying. They both preach a lot about our welfare and our future, but it seems to me that all the teachers are just slightly less messed up than the kids.

My greatest teacher tried to kill himself because he was afraid of telling people who he really was. He was the only one who made me feel like I belonged in this place, but I guess he didn't feel that close to me.

A horrible kid who used to try to rape me is dead, and I know I am a little bit at fault.

Mom's not coming back. She takes me on some weekends, and I don't bother to fight her any more. She pretends like we're adult friends. She never asks for any extra time. She doesn't want me. I don't know what's wrong with me to make my own mother feel like that. I don't think I will ever know.

Last night I had the same dream about Mr. Folsom that I had the night he tried to kill himself. Sometimes, when our new math teacher's droning on, there's a tiny flash of that same light Mr. Folsom was trying to show us. When that happens, I imagine it's a little star like those in my Folsom dream, and I pretend to add it to my dream collection. But there's nothing yet even close to the brightness of the moon.

Every school morning, as soon as my feet hit the pavement, I

...n to the head of the trail. Lucky runs up the slope and grabs me and I put my arms around his neck and he swings me completely around, just once. Then we talk to each other before anyone else can get into our day. He's happy now because he's going to live with his father. He loves me. I don't know how I could live without that. Lucky for me I don't have to.

TWK